Woodturning for Repair and Restoration

Woodturning for Repair and Restoration

A Practical Guide

Ian Wilkie

photography by

Nina Wilkie

The Crowood Press

First published in 1998 by
The Crowood Press Ltd
Ramsbury, Marlborough
Wiltshire SN8 2HR

British Library Cataloguing-in-Publication Data
A catalogue reference for this book is available from the British Library

ISBN 1 86126 128 4

Line illustrations by Andrew Green.

Acknowledgements
I would like to thank the following firms for their help and encouragement
over the years:

Ashley Iles
Axminster Power Tools Ltd
Chesterman
Crown Hand Tools Ltd
CSM Just Abrasives
GPS Agencies
Liberon
Multistar Machine & Tool Ltd
Peter Child
Record Power Tools Ltd
RTF Designs

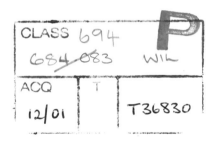

Typefaces used: text, New Baskerville and Garamond; headings, Optima Bold.

Typeset and designed by
D & N Publishing
Membury Business Park, Lambourn Woodlands
Hungerford, Berkshire.

Printed and bound by Paramount Printing Ltd, Hong Kong.

Contents

Fig. 1 The author turning a base on the faceplate.

Introduction

My primary aim in this book is to show you how to make use of your lathe and turning skills in a practical way to repair broken items. A turned leg here and a turned stretcher there can give a table or chair a new lease of life, and the result can be most satisfying and worth while. I have been involved from time to time in turning replacement parts for damaged furniture for collectors and antique dealers, and have learned some lessons along the way. The techniques and methods I describe and illustrate are by no means the only ones you could use, but this book is based very much on my own practical experience and how I personally have tackled various woodturning challenges. I hope you will enjoy using your lathe in this practical way – after all the lathe has many uses other than producing bowls and goblets!

In researching material for this book I have looked at many examples of antique furniture in National Trust properties, assessing how the item has been turned and how I could achieve the same shape. It becomes evident, as you begin to look more closely and become more observant, that furniture, clocks, fireplaces and ornaments have a surprising number of turned parts, and when you consider the equipment that was available when the piece was originally made one can only be humbled by the standard of the workmanship and the woodturning skills displayed. We are very fortunate to be able to see such good examples of fine work and all credit must go to such organizations as the National Trust.

One word of warning! If you are renovating a piece of furniture for a neighbour, friend, or member of the family do make sure that you know what you are doing. Discuss and sketch first what you both have in mind to avoid any disappointment and disagreement when the job is finished; it is amazing how misunderstandings can arise. You do not wish to be known as the person who wrecked Aunt Agatha's precious family heirloom! There is clearly a difference between a valuable, antique piece and an everyday, inexpensive item. With the former the rule is to replace only the very minimum possible: this may mean splicing on new wood and re-turning and I explain how this is done. Leave well alone if you think the task is beyond your skills. With a common or garden everyday item, it is probably wiser to restore the whole leg, stretcher or other part to make sure you have a strong and safe piece of woodwork that will not collapse at the first opportunity!

I have tried to keep the equipment as simple as possible and any average lathe will be quite suitable. In most chapters I have given instructions on how to make a complete basic replacement such as a knob, a leg or a handle, and then I have gone on to describe other examples and variations. It is highly unlikely that you will have a piece to repair with exactly the same measurements and diameters but in many cases the turning and holding techniques required will be similar, and the book will give you guidance on how to tackle your particular repair task.

1

The Lathe and Accessories

THE WOODTURNING LATHE

Most lathes on the market are quite suitable for the work described in this book. I have used a popular, inexpensive hobby lathe with 24in (60cm) between centres for the majority of the examples, and a lathe with 36in (90cm) between centres to turn longer handles and spindles. The distance between centres is often expressed without considering the drive centre in the headstock and the revolving centre in the tailstock, both of which reduce the effective distance between centres considerably. Turning long, narrow spindles can present problems of rigidity as the spindle tends to

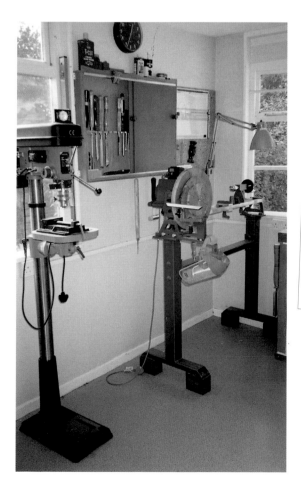

Lathe Requirements

In general it is important that the lathe should:

- be rigid and accurate
- take standard MT (morse taper) fittings in the headstock and tailstock
- have a hollow tailstock
- have an assortment of toolrests
- be able to take screw-on fittings on the headstock.

Fig. 2 Here is one of the lathes used in this book on its stand and a floor-standing drill press. The lathe is raised by wooden blocks to bring the centre height up to suit the author's height of 6ft (1.8m). There is plenty of natural light from two windows and an anglepoise lamp over the lathe for extra light. The cupboard with sliding doors houses the turning tools.

flex in the centre section. If the turner intends to undertake this type of turning regularly then a long bed lathe, together with an appropriate steady, would be required. If only the occasional long spindle is to be turned then turning the spindle in shorter lengths and joining may be the answer. When presented with a turning problem, there is often an ingenious solution and that is half the fun!

As lathes increase in price so does the degree of sophistication. On more expensive machines one would expect to find cam-action locking on the tailstock and toolrest assemblies, built-in indexing, a swivelling headstock, variable speed and a more powerful motor. Basically, however, if a lathe can hold piece of wood rigidly and rotate accurately, the rest is up to the skill of the turner!

LATHE ACCESSORIES

Holding is a very important part of turning. If the wood is not held firmly on the lathe then the whole turning process can be dangerous and the final result disappointing. Magazines and catalogues are filled with holding devices of one sort or another and the whole subject can be extremely confusing. No sooner have you made up your mind and decided on one system than another arrives on the scene claiming to be the ultimate in sophistication! The drives used and illustrated throughout this book have been chosen for their relative simplicity, accuracy, reliability and ease of use.

Wood can be held in a variety of ways for two distinct types of turning: **spindle** turning, where the wood is held between centres, and **faceplate** turning, where the

Fig. 3 A four-prong drive gripping a spindle firmly. When you purchase a new lathe, a four-prong drive is usually provided. The drive shown in the photograph has a sleeve that can be screwed forward to protect the turner from the sharp edges of the drive for safety.

wood is held on the headstock with no tail-stock support.

A new lathe is usually supplied with either a two- or four-prong drive, which fits into the MT hole in the headstock, and a solid (dead) centre, which fits in the MT hole in the tailstock. When turning a large-diameter item, such as a newel post, a prong drive is used because it bites into the wood, giving an effective grip, especially on woods such as pine. If a solid centre is used it is advisable to lubricate the end with wax or polish to avoid burning the wood while it is being turned.

With these basic accessories it will be possible to turn a prepared spindle be-tween centres, but there are many more accessories designed to help the turner and to make his job easier, and I have selected some that will be of particular use to the furniture repairer and are used throughout this book. Some turners advocate hammering small sections of wood directly into the MT spindle as a method of chucking but with small lathes this can damage the bearings and is not a practice I recommend.

RING CENTRE

This accessory is used in the headstock and offers three advantages for driving a spindle over the four-prong drive.

- It is safer to use as it has no sharp edges to catch tools or fingers
- If a 'dig-in' occurs the lathe will continue to revolve but the spindle will stop rotating, thus reducing the risk of the spindle flying off and causing an accident

Fig. 4 A ring centre leaves a clear indentation in the wood, which is an aid to remounting the blank should this be necessary. The photograph also shows a thread protector/ejector. The thread protector covers the headstock thread so that it cannot be damaged accidentally during turning. When the protector is screwed outwards it removes any MT fittings without the need for hammering them through the rear of the headstock spindle, thus protecting the bearings from damage.

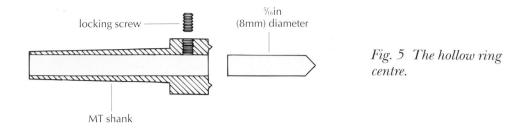

locking screw

⁵⁄₁₆in (8mm) diameter

MT shank

Fig. 5 The hollow ring centre.

- The centre leaves a clear ring indentation in the end of the wood, which makes it easy to remount the work accurately if it has been removed from the lathe for any reason.

Some ring centres are sold with adjustable or removable points. It is worth buying a good-quality ring centre because it will be used a great deal and the point can be resharpened. The centre can be used for holding pre-drilled blanks and when

drilling. It should be noted that this is a friction drive and it must be used with a revolving centre in the tailstock.

HOLLOW RING CENTRE

The hollow ring centre has a central pin with a parallel body usually ⁵⁄₁₆in (8mm) in diameter with a point ground at one end. The central pin is secured in the body by means of a hexagonal grub screw. The position of the point can therefore be adjusted

Fig. 6 A four-step Ian Wilkie friction drive.

Fig. 7 A lace bobbin drive designed to hold square spindles. The white dots on the drive and the spindle make realignment easy.

well beyond the ring so that ⅜in (10mm) or so of the parallel body is exposed. This can be used to support a pre-drilled blank. The wood is pushed firmly on to the pin until the ring is in contact with the end face of the wood.

THE STEPPED FRICTION DRIVE (FIG. 6)

This is a friction drive used in the head-stock, which I personally designed with four steps of ⅛, ¼, ⅜ and ⅝in (3, 6, 10 and 16mm) so it can be used to drive any spindle that has a hole matching one of these diameters. Because this is a friction drive the wood will cease to rotate if the turner digs in or makes a mistake, and this makes it a very safe accessory to use. There are no sharp edges to catch unwary hands or tool points. As the pre-drilled blank is held

between centres the final turned item will have an absolutely true centre hole. This feature is particularly important when making a light pull or curtain pull, to ensure that the finished pull hangs properly. It should be noted that as this is a friction drive, it must be used with a revolving centre in the tailstock.

LACE BOBBIN DRIVE

This drive is used in the headstock for driving small square-section spindles and for split turning.

REVOLVING CENTRE

This centre is used in the tailstock and consists of a MT shank and a body with one or more ballraces, which are designed to

13

Fig. 8 A multi-headed revolving centre, operated with two tommy bars with a number of different points. There are other inserts available, such as a small faceplate, ring centre and cone centre, which makes this type of revolving centre very versatile and ideal for restoration work.

allow the point of the centre to rotate. Some revolving centres have a variety of different replaceable points to cater for most types of turning. It is worth paying a little extra to buy a heavy-duty revolving centre with good bearings, which will withstand both axial and radial pressure.

FACEPLATE

The traditional method of holding work on to the headstock is with a faceplate. A faceplate screws directly on to the headstock spindle and has at least four countersunk holes in the back. The prepared blank to be turned is screwed to the plate with standard wood screws. It is useful to have both a 2in (5cm) and a 4in (10cm) faceplate. Good-quality faceplates are cast and machined so that they run absolutely true.

It is important to make sure that the wood screws used are the correct size, and that the blank is drilled with the right diameter pilot holes. Some trial and error is involved here. The first thing to do with a new faceplate is to make a register mark on the rim with a file so that if the work needs to be remounted at any stage it can be lined up with the mark to guarantee its concentricity. It is good practice to keep the faceplate, pilot drill and appropriate screws together in one place.

The disadvantage of screwing a blank directly to the faceplate is that the screw holes will be left in the finished work, which is not always acceptable; one way of overcoming this problem is to use a glue chuck and another is to use a jam chuck. Both these techniques are used throughout this book.

A **glue chuck** is made by securing a piece of wood to a faceplate, turning it to the round and facing it off. The prepared blank to be turned is then glued to the surface of the glue chuck. Superglues and hot-melt glues will give a virtually instant bond, but more time will be needed for PVA to cure.

Fig. 9 The faceplate.

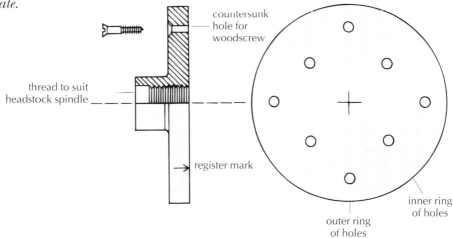

(Left) *Fig. 10 A standard cast-iron faceplate.*

A **jam chuck** is useful for holding partly turned items, spigots, frames or rings on a prepared wooden chuck, which in turn is held on a faceplate. After one face of the work has been completed, a wooden chuck is turned to match the recess or spigot exactly.

This jam chuck is screwed on to the faceplate; the partially turned work is reversed and literally 'jammed' on to the chuck so that the other surface can be turned. This method has the advantage that it leaves no indication of how the work was held.

SCREW CHUCK

A screw chuck is a device with a central screw which will hold a piece of wood securely on the headstock spindle ready for woodturning. All the turner needs to do is to drill a pilot hole of the correct diameter and depth in the centre of the wood blank to be turned. There are two main types of screw chuck: a simple dedicated screw chuck, which screws directly on to the headstock spindle and a screw chuck accessory, which can be fitted to a combination chuck.

A **dedicated screw chuck** is relatively inexpensive and can be used to hold wood for a wide range of turning operations. The disadvantage is that a hole is needed in the blank. This type of screw chuck has been available for many years and is produced in one form or another by a number of manufacturers. It consists of a steel body, threaded to suit various lathe spindles, and an integral faceplate of varying diameters,

in the centre of which a wood screw is fitted. Many of these chucks use a conventional, replaceable, No 14 wood screw, which is held in place by means of a backplate and a grub screw through the side of the chuck, which is designed to lock on to a filed flat on the side of the screw shank.

Other chucks have a machined screw with a parallel core, often in hardened steel. These parallel core screws can be more effective than conventional wood screws but on some chucks the screw has flat rather than sharp crests; in hardwoods the flat edge tends to crush the wood and so is less effective. The sharp-edged screw crest cuts into the wood rather like a metal thread-cutting tap, and it is possible to remount a blank at a later date with confidence, knowing that the work will run true.

The method of holding the screw into the body of the chuck is particularly important as the screw must be held centrally and absolutely firmly without any movement.

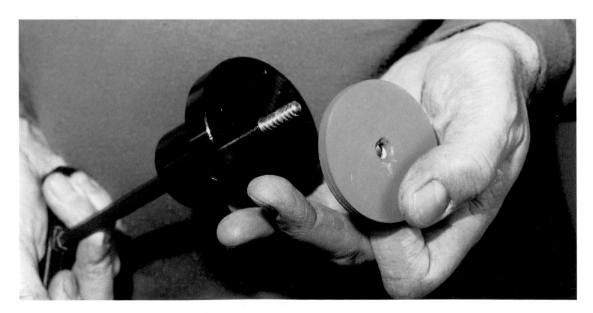

Fig. 11 A dedicated screw chuck. The home-made plywood spacer (painted green) protects the surface of the chuck and shortens the screw length by ¼in (6mm). The screw is tightened with the metal T-bar shown. A screw chuck is an easy way of holding a blank because only one hole is needed; I have used it for many tasks in this book.

The side grub screw method of holding often pushes the screw off its centre axis, and if a little grub screw is used alone there is often too much movement. One of the most effective screw chucks is a combined screw chuck and faceplate, which uses a high-tensile parallel core screw with nice crisp edges which is screwed in through the back of the chuck with the aid of a hefty hex spanner. The screw is absolutely central and there is no movement whatsoever. The face of the chuck is drilled to take four wood screws and can therefore also be used as a small faceplate.

An **accessory screw chuck** comes as an insert for a combination chuck, and varies in form and method of holding. The chuck insert is held in the chuck jaws in the compression mode. The trouble with screw chuck accessories is that they are an addition to the chuck and its jaws and therefore the overall rigidity may not always be as good as one might expect; moreover, if the chucks are not locked really tightly the whole assembly can rotate. The more moving parts are used, and the further the accessory is from the headstock spindle, the greater is the chance of vibration. In hefty, four-jaw centring chucks the screw chuck accessory is held quite firmly but the form of screw used in these chucks does differ considerably. When choosing a screw chuck test for possible movement of the screw, check the type, pitch and sharpness of the screw crest and look to see the method of securing the screw in the body.

It is important to take care when preparing the blank for the screw chuck. Always use the correct drill size to drill the pilot hole and store the drill with the chuck. The hole must be drilled at right angles so use a pillar drill or a drill in a drill-stand to ensure accuracy. It is a good idea to mark the twist drill with tape to act as a depth gauge. I recommend using a ply disc between the screw chuck and the blank in order to protect the face of the chuck and

I countersink the central hole on the outer face to ensure that the blank sits evenly on the face of the chuck. As you turn, remember where the screw is!

DRILL CHUCK (FIG. 12)

The quality and price of Jacob's-type drill chucks varies between expensive precision chucks and relatively cheap DIY chucks, which are quite adequate for most drilling in the lathe. More information about drilling and drill chucks is given in Chapter 4. The drill chuck is also useful for holding very small pieces of wood for turning.

COMBINATION CHUCK

If you are turning for a livelihood, a combination chuck that screws directly on to the headstock spindle will help you to carry out your turning operations quickly and efficiently. The amateur turner is not in such a hurry and can manage adequately with simple holding devices. That said, at some stage the turner will long to own a combination chuck because it is such an efficient piece of engineering.

A word of caution, however: if you are new to turning do not rush out to buy a chuck until you have some experience and an idea of what you want to turn. Many new turners find chucking systems and the accessories bewildering. It is expensive to change systems, so aim to choose the right one to suit your lathe first time! All these chucks are pricey and the wide range of possible additional accessories add to the cost. One chuck system will seldom do all the turner wants despite what the advertisers or the salesman would have you believe, but the more accessories used, the more complicated the chuck becomes to master. The more parts a chuck has, the more chance there is of vibration. The key to success in using combination chucks lies in the preparation of the wood blank prior to turning. If chucks are used

(Above) *Fig. 12 A drill chuck can be used to hold small, round blanks. Screw it directly on to the spindle thread. The chuck key must be removed before turning commences!*

Fig. 13 A typical combination chuck with its four metal jaw plates. These plates can be replaced with different-sized plates to suit the turner's needs.

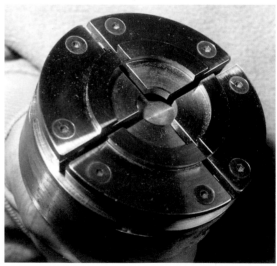

beyond their limits – that is, with the jaws protruding beyond the body – there is a greater chance of injury to the turner.

TOOLREST

A lathe usually comes with a standard length toolrest about 9in (23cm) long. An additional short toolrest 4in (10cm) long is also very useful to have. Extra-long toolrests are something of a luxury and invariably need a second tool-holder to go with them. They are very useful when turning long spindles but they are expensive.

STEADY

Proprietary steadies are an expensive purchase but may be a good investment if you intend to turn many long spindles. However, it is possible to manufacture a home-made device from inexpensive materials for the occasional task.

2

Turning Tools and How to Use Them

Today there is a bewildering number of turning tools of every size and shape available, many with very specialized uses. A basic set will be quite satisfactory for most of the work in this book. I am assuming in the descriptions below that the reader is right-handed: in each case the right hand controls the angle of the tool and is called the **control hand**, while the left hand steadies the tool and stops it from bouncing on the toolrest, and is referred to as the **steady hand**. For left-handed turners the instructions should be reversed.

ROUGHING-OUT GOUGE

A roughing-out gouge is primarily used for cutting away the wood on a square spindle, mounted between centres in the lathe, to form a cylinder. The tool can also be used for forming gentle convex and concave curves on a spindle. Most roughing-out gouges are forged into their curved shape from High Speed Steel (HSS) and then ground to give a bevel of 45 degrees. The most common size of roughing-out gouge is ¾in (19mm).

USING THE ROUGHING-OUT GOUGE

When presenting the tool to the wood keep the handle down and bring the heel of the tool gently into contact; swing the handle so that the bevel is in contact and then slightly further so that the cutting edge starts to cut the wood. Once the cutting

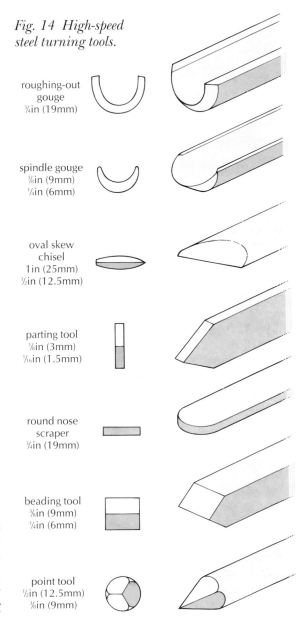

Fig. 14 High-speed steel turning tools.

roughing-out gouge ¾in (19mm)

spindle gouge ⅜in (9mm) ¼in (6mm)

oval skew chisel 1in (25mm) ½in (12.5mm)

parting tool ⅛in (3mm) ¹⁄₁₆in (1.5mm)

round nose scraper ¾in (19mm)

beading tool ⅜in (9mm) ¼in (6mm)

point tool ½in (12.5mm) ⅜in (9mm)

19

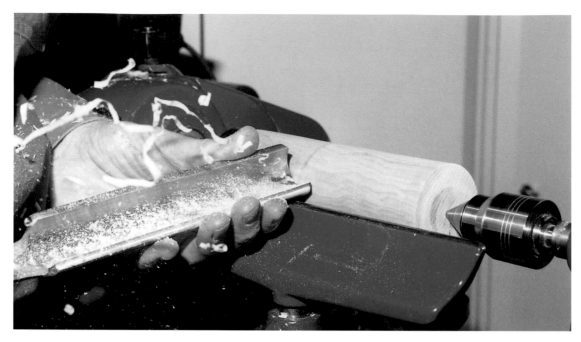

Fig. 15 The roughing-out gouge.

Fig. 16 The spindle gouge.

starts, move the tool along the toolrest, maintaining the same angle, so that a parallel cut is made. Always cut *off* the end of the wood not *into* it, so that the cutting edge has the support of the bevel. The closer the bevel is to the wood the finer the finish of the cut will be. Clearly the turner needs to be able to cut both left to right and right to left. Work from the centre outwards until the blank is round. Reposition the toolrest and turn from the centre outwards in the opposite direction to produce a cylinder.

SPINDLE GOUGE

A spindle gouge is primarily used for detailed shaping of a spindle. This is an easy tool to use and a very wide variety of shapes can be formed with it. The majority of gouges are ground from a solid HSS rod, which keeps its edge well, and the round cross-section means that the tool glides easily over the toolrest. The tool is ground with a bevel of between 45 and 60 degrees when viewed from the side, but the wings are ground back. Some turners grind the wings really far back, which increases the cutting edge. When viewed from the top the shape of the spindle gouge is similar to a finger nail and some of the smaller gouges are referred to as fingernail gouges. The most common tool size is the ⅜in (10mm), but the ¼in (6mm) size is also very useful. Most turners will probably have several sizes in their collection.

USING THE SPINDLE GOUGE TO CUT A 'V'

With the lathe rotating, draw a line on the wood with a pencil to represent the centre of the V. Position the toolrest on or slightly below the centre height. Hold the spindle gouge with the handle well down and approach the pencil line with the cutting edge of the tool, making sure that if a ruler

were placed across the tops of the flutes it would be vertical. The bevel should point in the direction of the required slope of the V. Take a gentle cut, withdraw the tool; reverse round the other way and repeat the procedure to form the other side of the V. Carry on cutting until the V is the desired shape and size. Keep the bevel close to the wood and always cut downhill, not uphill. It is important not to overcut at the bottom of the V or to allow the lower wing of the gouge to catch the other side of the V. This technique can also be used to form a chamfer on the end of a spindle, but obviously then you only need to work one way.

CUTTING A COVE

To cut a cove start as you would when making a V cut, but as the tool goes down into the wood, swing and lower the handle and twist the tool so that the flute is facing upwards at the bottom of the cut – that is, the bevel is close to the wood. In this way a curve will be formed. Repeat the process on the other side and vice versa until the desired cove is achieved. Watch the horizon of the spindle to see the shape.

CUTTING A GENTLE CURVE

Approach the wood with the heel of the tool and the handle well down. Gently swing the control hand to bring the bevel into contact with the wood and then swing the control hand further until the cutting edge begins to cut. Once the tool is cutting, the control hand can be swung still further to start a gently sloping downward cut. By moving the control hand, the cut can follow a convex or concave form. As the tool approaches the bottom of the cut make sure that the handle is twisted to bring the flute upwards and is held low to keep the bevel in contact with the wood. Be firm and positive, not hesitant! If you are too slow the tool will burn the wood.

PARTING TOOL

As its name implies, this tool is used for parting off work when turning has been completed, but it also has other uses. A ⅛in (3mm) tool is a useful size. There are different shapes available that are designed to reduce side friction, and these are usually ground in a diamond section. Another type, called the fluted parting tool, is designed to give a very crisp cut. A very thin parting tool with a ¹⁄₁₆in (1.5mm) blade is particularly useful for parting off expensive and exotic woods to avoid waste (*see* Fig. 18).

PARTING OFF

Parting off completely in the lathe by continuing the cut right through until the cutting point is exactly in the centre is a somewhat risky process. The wood might fly off, and if it is supported at the tailstock end it may well skew round and jam against the tool, giving the turner a fright! It is therefore suggested that the turner leaves at least a ¼in (6mm) spigot, which can be cut off with a fine-toothed hand saw once the wood is taken off the lathe. Do not be tempted to cut through the spigot with a hand saw in this way whilst the lathe is running, because if the blade jams it could cause an accident.

CUTTING A GROOVE

Place the toolrest on or slightly below the centre-line and close to the work. Rest the blade of the tool on the toolrest so that the cutting edge is parallel to the wood and the blade is vertical with the handle down. Bring the point of the tool up to the wood, and when it starts cutting into the surface push the blade into the wood and raise the control hand to continue the cut. The parallel shape of the tool causes friction, thus

Fig. 17 The ⅛in (3mm) parting tool.

Fig. 18 The very thin ¹⁄₁₆in (1.5mm) parting tool.

generating heat, so it is necessary to withdraw the tool after cutting into the surface about ¼in (6mm). Move the tool slightly along and repeat the process to widen the cut. Return to the first cut and repeat the process until the correct diameter is achieved. If you do not cut in small steps, the tool will become very hot and the wood will burn.

CUTTING A SPIGOT

One of the most common tasks for the parting tool is to produce a spigot. Use callipers to measure the diameter and start with a diameter that is slightly too large. The spigot can be increased in length, in steps, as required. It is important that the final cut produces a shoulder that is exactly at right angles to the wood so that the spindle will sit squarely in a hole and not show a gap when viewed from the side. If the

diameter of the selected drive is greater than the diameter of the spigot some waste wood will have to be left at the end, and an allowance for this must be made at the planning stage.

CUTTING A FILLET

The parting tool can be used to cut a fillet to enhance the crispness of the turning.

TRUING UP

Another use of the parting tool is to square up or true off an end. On very fine-grained wood, such as boxwood, the finish will be very good but on coarser-grained woods this may not be the case; however, if the end of the spindle is going into a hole, out of sight, this may not matter. The tool is used in the same way as when cutting a spigot but the depth of cut will vary.

Fig. 19 The oval skew.

THE SKEW CHISEL

With practice the skew enables the turner to produce a really smooth finish on spindles up to 4in (10cm) in diameter, whether parallel, tapered, or gently curved. I prefer the oval skew to the rectangular skew, and the 1in (25mm) oval skew, made from HSS, is a good, general-purpose turning tool. The oval skew is ground to the same angles as the rectangular skew: that is, 60 degrees when viewed from the top with 15-degree bevels when viewed from the side. Because of its shape it will pass over the toolrest without any edges that could catch and interrupt the even quality of cut. On the long point side there is usually a flat on the edge to ensure that the tool can be rested vertically on the toolrest when using the long point to cut a V or to square-off the end of a spindle. The edge on the short point side is rounded. Some turners do find the skew a difficult tool to use and talk nervously about dig-ins, but it is worth persevering!

USING THE SKEW

When I use the skew chisel I approach the wood with the *heel* of the tool, then lift the handle to bring the *bevel* into contact with the wood, and slightly twist the handle to bring the *cutting edge* into action. When the heel touches the wood nothing happens, when the bevel rubs against the wood only burnishing takes place; with the slight twist of the control hand the cutting edge starts to cut, but the bevel is then in place to offer support. Be positive and firm! If there is no bevel support and the long point is allowed to come into contact with the wood a dig-in can occur. It is always better to produce no cutting action when you approach a piece of wood rather than to cut too much or dig in.

FORMING AND SHAPING BALUSTERS

Twist the control hand to cut downhill from the left to the right to form a gentle curve to the shoulder. This means that the final cut is made with the short point. It is much better to make a number of light cuts rather than a few big ones, and so gradually develop the shape. The oval chisel shape makes it easier to control the cut. Always cut down the slope; if the turner attempts to cut up a slope he will lose control of the tool.

PRODUCING A CRISP 'V' CUT

To form a V cut the skew is held with the handle well down and the flat on the tool-rest with the long point just touching the wood. The blade must be held vertically. Push the tool into the wood to form a shallow V. To widen the V, hold the tool with one bevel pointing down the slope required and push the tool gently down into the V to form the side. The process is repeated on the other side. Make several light cuts until the desired V is formed.

SQUARING OFF THE ENDS OF SPINDLES

Hold the tool with the handle down and the long point just touching the wood, with the bevel rubbing. Push the tool in to make very gentle cuts. The flat on the edge of the long point will help to keep the blade vertical.

FORMING BEADS

A bead is formed by cutting two Vs to an equal depth with the long point of a skew, and then rounding off the centre area. A pencil line in the centre between the V cuts helps to achieve symmetry. Be careful not to take wood away from the centre or the bead will be too small. Develop the sides of the bead with a number of cuts rather than a single cut. Form the left-hand side of the bead first. Always ensure that the bevel is supporting the cutting edge and take gentle cuts; always cut downhill.

THE SCRAPER

The scraper has no place in spindle turning; it is primarily used for finishing cuts on bowls and platters and for this it is very useful. The tool consists of a carbon steel or HSS blade, ground with a bevel of 45 degrees to the profile required. Some turners prefer a bevel of 70–75 degrees. A ¾in (19mm) scraper is a useful size for general-purpose work. The cutting action is at the edge of the tool, where a burr is formed rather like that found on the conventional cabinet scraper. The arises on the bottom of the blade should be slightly rounded off

Fig. 20 Scrapers can be ground to different shapes to suit individual needs.

to reduce the risk of the tool catching on the toolrest. The shape can be ground to suit individual needs.

USING THE SCRAPER

The scraper is held in the same manner as other conventional turning tools, but, unlike with other tools, the handle is held *up* and not *down* so that the cutting edge of the tool is in the trailing position. If the handle is held down there is a risk that if the cutting edge is caught by the grain of the wood it could be pulled down and into the wood, causing a dig-in. With the handle up, should the grain catch the cutting edge, the edge of the tool will be pulled down and *away* from the surface of the wood, reducing the likelihood of a dig-in. The secret of a good, clean cut is a firm but gentle movement with a sharp tool. With care the scraper will give a good, level cut, and it can be used to remove any unevenness left by the gouge.

ADDITIONAL TURNING TOOLS

There are a number of specialist, and often innovative, tools always appearing on the market. They tend to be expensive but could be of interest to the repairer or restorer. Most work can be carried out with the tools listed above although I have added below two other tools that I have used and illustrated in this book.

BEADING TOOL

The beading tool is similar in shape to a parting tool but is ground from square stock and is useful for turning small beads, as its name suggests. It can also be used to hollow out wood to form a socket to take a spigot. Two sizes are useful: the ⅜in (10mm) and the ¼in (6mm).

POINT TOOL

The point tool is ground from round stock with three facets, and can be used for cutting decorative grooves, forming beads and squaring off ends in hard, close-grained woods. The tool is usually ground from ⅜in (10mm) to ½in (13mm) HSS stock and fitted with a short, relatively stubby handle. This tool was initially designed to turn boxwood and ivory in the last century and has recently been rediscovered. Some point tools are ground from diamond-section stock, but these are less easy to use than those made from round stock.

Home-made Tools

HSS turning tools sold by leading manufacturers are made to exacting standards and represent good value for money. There is always a temptation to convert old files, or carbon steel chisels bought at a jumble sale, into turning chisels. The problem with this is producing a tool that has the correct temper at each part of its length, for which a thorough, specialist knowledge of the heat treatment of metal is essential. A file is very brittle and often has a very short tang, so there is a risk that a tool made from a file could snap, causing injury to the turner. Because tools are relatively cheap, the turner is urged to buy the tool designed for the job and not to try to get by using cheap ones. I would rather have five basic, good-quality HSS chisels than twenty bargain, doubtful ones!

3

Sharpening

It is vital to keep turning tools sharp, and the turner will need to invest in a bench grinder. The choice of machines is wide, but when deciding which is the best buy for your particular needs, bear in mind that this is a potentially dangerous machine with two heavy grindstones rotating at 3,000rpm; on to these wheels you will place steel tools, generating sparks and metal and abrasive dust. This is a machine that must be treated with respect! You want a safe, solid, reliable machine that can be easily secured to a bench or table and that has adjustable toolrests that lock firmly.

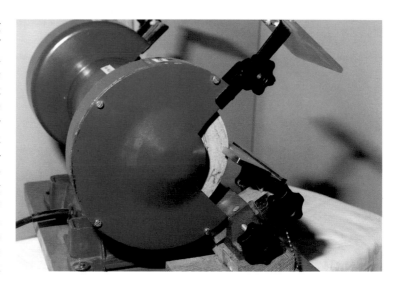

Fig. 21 View of the grindstone with its white wheel in position. Note the toolrest, which is an addition to the basic grinder. The toolrest can be set accurately to the angle required and is a valuable addition to any grinder.

THE PARTS OF A BENCH GRINDER

MOTOR

The machine has a motor with an arbor at each end. Check that the motor carries a CE rating and that it is quiet in operation.

PROTECTIVE COVER

This guard must cover at least 70 per cent of the wheel to ensure protection to the operator should the wheel disintegrate for some reason. Do not operate the machine with the guard removed.

SPARK GUARD

The spark guard is a metal plate positioned at the top of the protective cover opening, which should be set at not more than ³⁄₁₆in (5mm) from the cutting surface of the stone. The spark guard should always be in position.

PROTECTION SCREENS

The screens are made from clear perspex or armoured glass and are sited above each wheel; their purpose is to protect the user against flying grit and metal filings, and should always be in position.

TOOLRESTS

Toolrests are adjustable and should be set no more than ⅛in (3mm) from the cutting surface of the stone. The toolrest supplied with a machine is often flimsy and awkward to set. It is well worth removing at least one of the toolrests and replacing it with a stronger and better-designed model; these are available as accessories.

GRINDSTONES

Most machines have two grindstones, one mounted on each arbor. The stones are held between two flanges, which should be at least one-third of the diameter of the wheel, and they are secured by a nut with a left-handed thread on the left side and a right-handed thread on the right side, when viewed from the front. A grindstone of at least 6in (15cm) diameter and ¾in (19mm) width is recommended; the wider the stone is the better, but bear in mind that each model of bench grinder is designed to take only a particular diameter and width of wheel. One of the stones should be a white stone, which is intended for grinding HSS.

DRESSING A STONE

After a while, metal filings become embedded in the surface of the wheel and this is known as **glazing**. The wheel may also become uneven. If the metal is allowed to build up on the surface and not removed, the cutting efficiency of the stone will be reduced and the friction will be increased; this in turn causes excessive heat on the cutting edge of the tool. One of the advantages of the white stone is that the metal particles embedded in the surface are clearly visible, which is not the case with a grey stone. To remove the metal particles, the wheel is dressed with either a devil stone, a star wheel dresser or a diamond dresser. All

Fig. 22 Dressing and cleaning a white wheel with a diamond dresser.

these devices are relatively inexpensive, the diamond dresser being the dearest. The devil stone is made of material which is harder than the stone to be dressed; it is passed over the rotating wheel, cleaning and flattening the surface. The other devices are used in a similar way. Dressing a stone can be a particularly dusty operation, especially with a devil stone, and therefore it is advisable to wear goggles and a mask and to use an extraction system.

SHARPENING YOUR TOOLS

It is essential to keep turning tools sharp! Blunt tools are dangerous and will produce unsatisfactory work.

THE ROUGHING-OUT GOUGE

This is best sharpened on a 6in (15cm) bench grinder fitted with a white wheel for HSS. It is important not to round off the wings of the tool and for this reason I grind the two wings first and then the curved section between. I usually remove the burr

Safety Rules when Operating a Bench Grinder

- Treat the machine with respect
- Always wear eye protectors when operating a bench grinder and ensure that they are marked EN166, which is the current EC standard
- If you suspect that the stone is cracked or damaged, suspend it from a horizontally held pencil and tap it lightly on the side. It should give a clear ringing sound; if a dull thud is heard, it probably means that the stone is damaged and should not be used
- Only the front surface of the wheel should be used, not the sides. Using the sides can damage the wheel and any weakening of the sides of a stone that rotates at high speed could have disastrous results!
- Never use the machine without the protective screens in position
- Never use the machine without the spark guard more than ³⁄₁₆in (5mm) from the grinding wheel
- Ensure that the toolrest is not more than ⅛in (3mm) from the grinding surface
- Bolt the grinder down on to a bench or table
- Keep the workshop tidy. Sparks falling on wood shavings, oily rags, wire wool or inflammable materials, such as polish, may start a fire
- It is sensible to wear a mask when grinding and particularly when dressing a stone

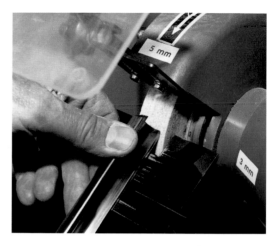

Fig. 23 Keep the guards in position and make sure that the toolrest is set no more than ⅛in (3mm) from the cutting surface of the stone. The spark guard fitted to the upper edge of the wheel guard should be adjusted so that it is no more than ³⁄₁₆in (5mm) from the stone. Never use the sides of the stone!

Fig. 24 Sharpening the roughing-out gouge. Before sharpening the tool, cover the bevel with felt pen; this will help to indicate which part of the bevel has been ground away.

from the inside of the flute with a slip-stone, taking care not to rock the slipstone over the top edge.

THE SPINDLE GOUGE

This should be sharpened on a bench grinder. The front angle should be about 45 degrees, and the wings of the gouge should be ground back by moving the gouge gently up the wheel and rotating the handle to the right or to the left as appropriate. The burr left on the inside of the tool can be removed with a slipstone. In sharpening there is a tendency to grind the end so that it becomes pointed; this should be avoided if possible, because it will be difficult to turn good round coves with a pointed end.

THE PARTING TOOL

This is relatively easy to sharpen, compared to other chisels. When you buy a new tool the blade is usually ground to the correct angle and all that is needed in the first instance is to run the tool over the oilstone to give a really crisp cutting edge. On some tools the edges of the blade (the arises) are sharp and can catch on the toolrest; gentle application of an oilstone, or a slipstone, can round these arises off. The cutting edge can be maintained on an oilstone, and if the tool needs regrinding at some stage it can be ground on the bench grinder with a white wheel, although I find it easier to regrind this tool on a disc sander.

THE OVAL SKEW

This tool only needs honing on an oilstone, DMT or ceramic tile to give a really sharp edge. To do this, place the tool with one bevel flat on the stone, with one finger on the top bevel to reduce the risk of the lower bevel rocking, and pull the chisel across the stone towards you. Two or three sweeps will form a wire edge that can be clearly felt with a finger or seen by those with good eyesight. Then turn the tool over and do the same on the other bevel so that a wire edge is formed on the other side. Repeat the process until

Fig. 25 Honing an oval skew on a diamond stone. Keep the bevel flat on the stone and draw the skew backwards. Make sure that the bevel is kept flat on the stone and not rocked.

the wire edge finally breaks off, leaving a sharp edge. For really crisp turning, carry out the same sequence on a leather strop that has been dressed with fine carborundum valve-grinding paste. After a time the flats at the cutting edge and at the heel will gradually get longer; if they are too long it can be quite hard to form a wire edge. This is the time to regrind the tool.

THE SCRAPER

The scraper needs to be sharpened regularly, and to do this, first rub the top surface over a flat oilstone, ceramic stone or DMT, keeping the tool flat on the stone to remove the blunted burr. Grind the tool to an angle of 45 degrees on the bench grinder using a toolrest. The tool will now have a burr on the top and is ready for use. An alternative method is to use a proprietary burnisher designed for this specific purpose.

THE BEADING TOOL AND THE POINT TOOL

These tools can be kept sharp on an oilstone, ceramic stone or DMT.

4

Drills and Saws

The woodturner needs to be able to drill pilot holes for a screw chuck or a faceplate, but there are many other cases where a hole will be required, for instance to take a spigot, for an electric wire in a lamp, in handles to take a tang, for spaced holes in hubs, wheels and axles and so on.

THE DRILL PRESS

Most woodworkers will, at the very least, have a power drill and many will possess a drill press, although some stalwarts still rely on a hand drill or a brace and bit. The turner needs to be able to drill a wide variety of holes, of different diameters and depths, often at right angles, with a reasonable degree of accuracy. Drilling can be done off the lathe, or in some circumstances on the lathe. Although the power drill in a drill stand can be quite adequate, accuracy may be a problem. There is often play in the drill's bearings and an unacceptable sideways movement because the drill is held in the drill stand by means of its 1¾in (45mm) collar, which is invariably part of the plastic casing of the drill. For accuracy and rigidity a dedicated drill press is a better option. When selecting a drill press there are various points to consider, discussed below.

BENCH OR FLOOR-STANDING MODEL?

This decision will probably be determined by the size of your workshop, how much you wish to spend and the maximum length you require between the table and the end of the drill bit. If you intend to do

Fig. 26 A power drill held in a drill stand with a machine vice bolted on to the table.

much restoration work you would be wise to choose a floor-standing model so that you can drill the ends of table legs, newel posts and so on.

SPINDLE TRAVEL

The spindle travel figure refers to the maximum plunge that the drill can achieve in one go without moving the work. In small drills this is usually 2in (5cm) but rises up to a maximum of 5in (13cm) in bigger drills.

POWER

If the drill is to be used for drilling large holes and for heavy work then the power of the motor becomes a significant factor.

THROAT DEPTH

This is the distance from the centre line of the spindle to the column. This measurement will determine the maximum diameter of wood blank that can be drilled in the centre – that is, the swing.

SPEED

Drill presses usually offer a range of speeds. The general rule to go by is: the harder the wood, the slower the speed, and the larger the diameter, the slower the speed.

RACK AND PINION MECHANISM

The table, especially when fitted with a machine vice, can be a heavy item to move up and down the column, and therefore it is a considerable advantage if the drill is fitted with a rack and pinion mechanism to raise and lower the table.

ENGINEERING AND FINISH

Look to see that the castings, levers and rack and pinion are all well made and that the paintwork is good quality.

ACCESSORIES

Check especially what mortise attachments are available, as these can be useful for restoration work.

MACHINE VICES

A really good-quality machine vice, designed for engineering work, is very expensive, but

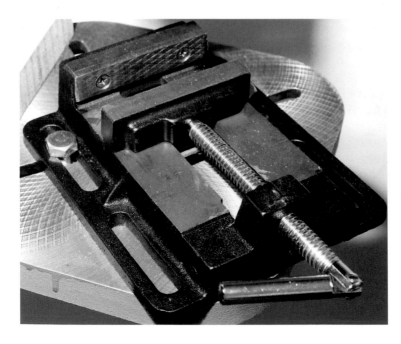

Fig. 27 A machine vice should be used on the table of the drill press for holding wood securely ready for drilling. Do not be tempted to hold the wood by hand, as this can cause injury if the drill binds in the hole and the wood spins round at high speed.

fortunately there are a number of relatively inexpensive vices available that are ideal for the woodworker. A vice is used to hold the work on the table firmly, safely and accurately during the drilling operation, and it is important that it can be secured to the table with bolts. If a machine vice or a clamping device is not used, and the drill binds in the hole, a nasty accident can occur.

TYPES OF DRILL BIT
STANDARD JOBBER'S DRILL BITS

The woodturner is likely to have a selection of standard twist bits from 1/16 to 3/8in (1.5mm to 10mm) diameter and these sizes will cater for drilling pilot holes for chucks and faceplates. Most twist drills are now HSS but some will be made from softer carbon steel, which is suitable for wood although HSS will keep its edge much longer, particularly if the drills are used for drilling both wood and metal. Twist drills are available in an incredible range of sizes in both metric and imperial measurements. Sets of drill bits look really attractive, but it is probably wiser to buy drills singly as and when they are required. Extra-long drills can be purchased for particular needs, such as for drilling light pull blanks; a typical 1/4in (6mm) twist drill measures 3½in (9cm) overall in length whereas a similar diameter extra-long drill measures 5½in (14cm). For twist drills above 3/8in (10mm) the price increases considerably, and the woodturner would be well advised to look at other forms of drill bit for drilling larger holes. Twist drills have parallel shanks and can therefore only be used in drill chucks.

BULLET DRILL BITS

There have been a number of innovations in twist drills over the last few years in response to the increased popularity of modern,

Safety when Drilling

- Always wear eye protection
- Always use a chuck guard
- Make sure the wood is held firmly in a machine vice or cramped to the table
- Use sharp drill bits
- Make sure that the bit is securely held in the chuck
- Never leave the chuck key in the chuck
- Bolt the machine down
- Keep hands away from the rotating drill
- Do not run the machine with the belt guard open
- Beware the end of the drill bit, as it can get very hot!
- Always remember that you are using a powerful machine, driving a sharp cutting tool at high speed, so the machine needs to be handled with respect!

portable drills. The bullet point drill bit remains sharp for much longer than the standard drill bit, produces a more precise hole without splintering the wood and is equally effective for drilling metals and plastics. These drills are available from 1/8in to 3/8in (3mm to 10mm) in half sizes and they cost twice the price of a standard twist drill.

LIP AND SPUR DRILL BITS

These are precision drill bits available in a range of sizes from 1/8 to 1¼in (3mm to

33

Fig. 28 A saw-toothed Forstner bit being used to drill a central hole in a base. The wood being drilled in this case was temporarily glued to a piece of scrap ply with hot-melt glue, and the ply was cramped to the table.

32mm), and are designed only for drilling wood. The drills are ground with a single centre point and two outer cutting spurs. The centre point allows the bit to be positioned precisely on a previously marked spot before drilling commences and will stop the drill from wandering. The suppliers of these drills claim that they are best drills of their type made anywhere in the world today. They are available in a range of sizes from ⅛ to 1¼in (3mm to 30mm) and cost half as much again as the standard twist bits.

FLAT BITS

The cheapest option, when drilling large holes, is to use a flat bit, but this would not be my own choice. I personally find that

the centre point tends to be too long and that the drill vibrates and chatters.

FORSTNER BITS

The Forstner saw tooth bit cuts a good, smooth hole, provided that the shavings are cleared frequently and not allowed to build up; quite a deep hole can be drilled. The reader will often see attractively boxed sets of Forstner bits at special offer prices but I prefer to have a few that I know are of really good quality. I have standardized on just four sizes: ½, ⅝, ¾ and 1in (13, 16, 19 and 25mm).

EXPANDING BITS

For holes of an unusual size, which are sometimes required in restoration work for example, I use an expanding bit. Although the bit is calibrated, some trial and error on scrap wood, to get the correct diameter first, is recommended.

Flat bits, Forstner bits and expanding bits are all used in a drill chuck.

DRILLING TECHNIQUE USING THE DRILL PRESS

1. Either cramp the work securely to the table, or better still use a machine vice. For repetitive drilling, a home-made jig, in conjunction with a cramp or a machine vice, is often required.
2. First pop the hole position to be drilled with a punch to act as a guide for the drill bit.
3. When drilling right through a piece of wood, place a scrap piece under the work to reduce the risk of splintering as the drill breaks through, and to eliminate the possibility of drilling into the table.
4. Small-diameter drills can 'lead off' as they follow the grain, and will therefore not run true if the tendency is not corrected; furthermore, the drill bit can break. The solution is to ensure firstly that the drill bit is sharp and secondly to take time drilling the hole.
5. Should the drill show signs of overheating or burning the wood, stop the machine and reduce the speed.
6. Allow the drill to cut without applying too much downward pressure.
7. Bring the drill out of the hole every so often to clear the shavings. With some hardwoods the flutes quickly become clogged, especially when drilling deep holes, so they need to be cleaned or the bit may break.
8. Use the calibrated depth stop that is built in.

DRILLING IN THE LATHE

Successful drilling in the lathe presupposes that the headstock and tailstock line up perfectly, which, alas, is not always the case. I am not very keen on drilling central holes in wood mounted on the lathe for this reason, and wherever possible I drill in the drill press; the exception is long-hole boring, and indexed and angled drilling.

LONG-HOLE BORING

An auger, a counterbore and a hollow ring centre are required to carry out long-hole boring. The most common auger and counterbore size is $\frac{5}{16}$in (8mm). Augers are usually 30in (76cm) in length, but when a handle is fitted this is reduced by up to 4in (10cm); moreover, when the auger is passed through the tailstock the length of the drill can be decreased by a further 8in (20cm). The counterbore needs to be fitted with a $\frac{3}{16}$in (5mm) parallel pin to match the auger. This tool is held in the headstock to drive the work after the first half of the spindle has been drilled and then reversed on the lathe. Some counterbores have pins or a pointed centre for use as a conventional four-prong drive. The ring centre allows you to feed the auger through the tailstock and into the revolving work. If your lathe does not have a hollow tailstock, a boring jig that locks in the tool post holder will be required. If you want to drill really long spindles, this boring jig is a worthwhile accessory because it is shorter than the average tailstock, giving you a greater reach.

Method
1. Mount the spindle to be drilled in the lathe with a four-prong drive in the headstock and a hollow ring centre in the tailstock.
2. Spin the spindle, increasing the tailstock pressure, until the ring centre has

Fig. 29 An auger is passed through the hollow tailstock to bore a long hole. Note the hollow centre fitted in the tailstock quill with a large cut-out area on its side, which allows the wood shavings to be ejected and thus reduces the tendency of the auger to bind and jam in the hole.

made a firm impression on the end of the wood.

3. Stop the lathe and remove the centre pin and the grub screw from the ring centre.
4. Pass the auger through the end of the hollow tailstock spindle and commence drilling. Drill only very short sections, no more than ⅛in (6mm) at a time. Withdraw the auger completely after drilling each section to clear away the waste, otherwise the auger can bind or overheat. Drill halfway through the wood.
5. Replace the four-prong drive with the counterbore fitted with a pin to match the diameter of the auger. Reposition the centre pin in the hollow ring centre and secure it with the grub screw. Mount the part-drilled spindle with the hole on the counterbore. Once again increase the pressure on the tailstock and run the lathe for the ring centre to cut an impression. Stop the lathe and remove the centre point and the grub screw.
6. Continue drilling with the auger until the two holes meet.

Possible Problems and Solutions
• The two holes do not meet. This is sometimes because the auger is too flexible or too blunt and has wandered and followed the grain in the wood
• The auger jams in the hole. Turn off the lathe and pull out the auger. The jamming has probably happened because wood dust has built up in the hole. Only drill short sections at a time
• The wood burns. This is caused by the auger overheating. Only drill short sections at a time
• The spindle flexes. A long spindle will need to be supported by a steady device

INDEXED AND ANGLED DRILLING

There are proprietary guides for drilling accurately spaced holes into the side of, or into the face of, wood on the lathe. The holes can be drilled at any angle. A chuck with an indexing facility will also be needed. Such a guide is useful for drilling holes in wheels or hubs, for example.

THE JACOB'S DRILL CHUCK

These chucks are available to take drills with shanks of up to ¾in (19mm) diameter; the average-sized Jacob's chuck is designed to take ½in (13mm) diameter drills. The back of the chuck body will either have a

Fig. 30 A drilling guide can be used with a power drill for drilling holes on the face, or the side, of work in the lathe.

Fig. 31 Drilling a centre hole in a handle with the drill chuck in the headstock. Note that the end of the handle is supported in a cup-shaped insert fitted into a multi-head revolving centre in the tailstock.

Jacob's taper hole, 1 to 6, or a threaded hole. To use the drill chuck in the head-stock or the tailstock of the lathe a MT shank that has the correct fitting for the chuck will be required. The threads do vary. On some chucks the thread size, or the Jacob's taper size, is engraved on the body, but if there is any doubt take the chuck with you to make sure you purchase the right MT shank. The chucks are oper-ated by means of a key, which is used to tighten the three self-centring jaws. The quality and price varies from expensive precision chucks to relatively cheap DIY chucks, which are quite adequate for most drilling in the lathe. There are two ways of using the drill chuck in the lathe, with it held either in the headstock or tailstock.

Drill Chuck in the Headstock
With this method the wood is held station-ary. The revolving drill bit bores into the wood as the tailstock is advanced. This method may usefully be used for drilling a hole in a handle to take the tang of a tool, for example.

Drill Chuck in the Tailstock

Here the drill is held stationary in the tail-stock, while the wood is mounted on the headstock. The wood revolves and the static drill is advanced into the wood. This method might be used to drill a hole to take a spigot.

Fig. 32 The drill chuck fitted in the tailstock.

Possible Problems

- If the drill binds in the wood, the chuck and its MT shank may start to rotate in the tailstock spindle
- When withdrawing the drill from the wood the MT shank may work loose from the tailstock and start to rotate

Possible Solutions

One solution is physically to hold the chuck body with one hand as it is advanced or withdrawn from the wood. If the chuck has any sharp edges this can be a risky business, and most turners would not feel comfortable doing this. I prefer to use a draw-bar, which screws into

Fig. 33 If a drill chuck is to be used in the headstock to hold small items, there is always a risk that the MT shank will work loose during the turning; a draw bar passed through the outboard end of the spindle and screwed into the end of the MT will stop this happening.

Fig. 34 Drill chucks can be purchased with a screw thread to match that of the lathe spindle. This cuts out the need for a draw bar, but these chucks tend to be much more expensive than a chuck and a draw bar.

Fig. 35
The two-wheel bandsaw.

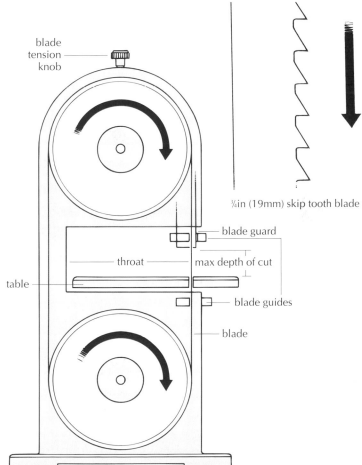

blade tension knob

¾in (19mm) skip tooth blade

blade guard

throat — max depth of cut

table

blade guides

blade

the end of the MT shank, passes through the head-stock or tailstock and is secured by means of a cone nut. Most lathes do have a hollow tailstock but unfortunately not all have a hollow headstock. If this is the case with your lathe, your best solution is to purchase a threaded drill chuck, which screws directly on to the headstock spindle

THE BANDSAW

The bandsaw is one of the most useful machines in the workshop and is a must for the serious woodturner. There are two sorts of band-saw: the three-wheeled and the two-wheeled. When it comes to choosing a band-saw the turner would be wise to take a long-term view and to invest in the largest two-wheel machine that he can afford. The smaller three-wheel bandsaws can be disappointing, and will certainly not cope with large sections of heavy timber. A bandsaw with a 12in (30cm) throat, a capacity of 6–8in (15–20cm) depth of cut, and one that will take blades from ¼ to ¾in (6–19mm), will meet most needs.

An adjustable parallel fence is essential and a calibrated mitre fence is a very useful accessory. A bandsaw creates a great deal of dust so a model with an extraction point to attach a dust extractor has a distinct advantage.

The blades used in the machine are hard-point blades and when blunt are disposed of rather than sharpened. My own saw is permanently fitted with a ¾in (19mm) skip tooth, hard-point 4tpi blade, which is actually designed for the meat and fish trade. A blade such as this will cut straight lines in timber up to 8in (20cm) thick with no trouble, and will cut down to veneer thickness. To ensure a good cut it is important that the blade guides are set accurately and that the blade is replaced when it becomes blunt.

CUTTING WITH THE BANDSAW

This machine is capable of cutting both straight and curved lines. I use my bandsaw primarily for cutting straight lines to produce turning blanks for spindle work. When I require a round blank I simply cut the corners off a rectangle rather than cut a circle. It is not difficult to make a special one-off jig to hold a particularly awkwardly shaped piece of wood in order that it can be cut safely.

When cutting very small pieces of wood it is a good idea temporarily to glue the timber to a larger piece of waste wood before putting it through the saw. Hot-melt glue is particularly useful for this task. I use this technique when I am cutting expensive or exotic woods.

Safety Rules when Using the Bandsaw

- Disconnect the machine when changing or adjusting blades
- Concentrate when cutting and try to avoid disturbances
- Make sure that there is plenty of room in the workshop to manoeuvre the timber
- Only expose enough bandsaw blade to cut the thickness of the wood
- Keep fingers well away from the blade
- Use a push stick
- When cutting branch wood, or a round section blank, make a cradle to hold the wood so that the branch does not swing round and damage the blade
- Do not use the bandsaw for cutting small pieces of wood that could equally well be cut in seconds with a small hand saw.
- If the wood is old or reconstituted check that there are no hidden nails, screws, bits of iron, or even stone, embedded in the wood, which would damage the bandsaw blade
- Wear eye protection and a dust mask when operating the bandsaw

Make a push stick to help to guide the wood into the blade. In this way you can keep your fingers well away from the blade.

5

Wood and Adhesives

PREPARING BLANKS FOR TURNING

Wood can be prepared by hand but this can be time-consuming and hard work! Time spent preparing timber ready to be put on the lathe is time well spent. A correctly prepared blank will be much easier to mount on the lathe and faults, cracks and unacceptable knots become more obvious. An uneven, badly balanced piece of wood can place strain on the lathe bearings and be quite intimidating to turn! Cutting or planing off the corners of large, round blanks of hardwood first to make them roughly round makes roughing out easier.

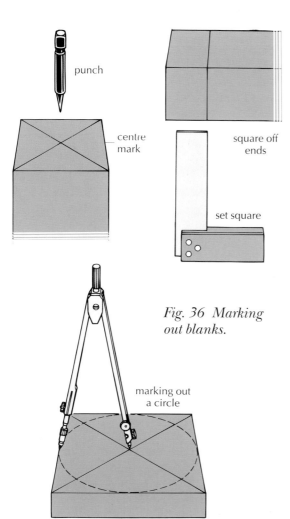

Fig. 36 Marking out blanks.

MARKING UP

Before the prepared blank can be mounted on the lathe it will need to be marked up accurately and the centres punched. The turner will need a pencil, straight edge, tri-square, Vernier callipers and a pair of compasses together with a punch and hammer. Proprietary centre finders are also very useful.

To mark the centre on the ends of a prepared spindle draw two diagonal lines from opposite corners. The centre point should then be punched with a steel punch so that the spindle can be aligned accurately in the lathe. A round blank will already have a centre point made by the compass point.

SELECTING WOOD

It is always difficult to match wood, and even if you can identify the original wood, merely obtaining a piece of the same species will not necessarily result in a perfect match. For example, mahogany includes a huge range of different types of wood from all over the world with varying colours, textures, weights and turning properties. When it comes to trying to find wood suitable for a repair or restoration task you have to accept that the wood will need staining, and therefore it is best to try to match the grain and texture of the host item as closely as possible rather than worry too much about an exact colour match. The following woods are all ones that I have used and found suitable for turning. Staining wood is covered in Chapter 6.

WOOD

HOME-GROWN WOODS

Ash
Ash is mainly white in colour but often has a heart of light brown. The wood is very tough and elastic with a coarse texture. It finishes very well and seldom splits, making it a good choice for handles, shafts and legs.

Beech
This timber has a fine, close, grain and an even texture and it takes stain very well. It is moderately hard and heavy. Beech turns extremely well and can be used for knobs, handles, feet, legs and similar items. It is not recommended for exterior use and it is prone to worm attack.

Box
Boxwood is a very finely grained hardwood, with a colour varying from cream to golden yellow to light brown, with dark-brown streaks. This timber is very easy to work and takes a good finish and high polish. It cuts, turns, drills and glues exceptionally well. Traditionally, box has been used by woodworkers for chess pieces, wood engraving blocks, inlay work, tool handles, some small kitchen utensils, measuring instruments – indeed, for anything that requires a fine, evenly textured, straight-grained wood.

Cherry
This is a hard, heavy and tough wood with a fine, even, texture and is ideal for attractive handles for items such as warming pans and for knobs and feet. It takes stain well. Like most fruitwoods, cherry is pleasant to turn.

Sweet Chestnut
This timber resembles oak and is often used as a substitute for it, although it does not have the distinctive rays found in oak. It is hard and durable but lighter in weight than oak. It turns extremely well and can be used for legs, balustrades and so on.

Holly
Holly is white in colour and has a very fine texture. It is a difficult wood to season but when seasoned well it is ideal for small turned items such as chessmen and knobs. It stains well and can be used as a substitute for ebony.

Hornbeam
This wood is yellowish-white in colour. It is hard, heavy, strong and tough. It is used for small turned items such as handles and for mechanical items such as cogs and cams for automata.

Oak
Oak is light brown in colour, hard, heavy and very strong and durable. The wood hardens and darkens with age and it can be cut to give a beautiful grain pattern. Oak turns well and can be used for legs, feet and knobs, newel posts and balusters.

Pear
This timber is pink to red in colour with a very fine grain and texture but with little apparent figure, and rather bland. It is excellent for turning, particularly when carving is to be added. It takes stain very well and can be used to simulate woods such as ebony.

Sycamore

This timber comes from one of the largest European maples and it is hard, heavy and strong with a uniform grain and close texture, which gives a smooth and lustrous finish. The wood is white and is used extensively in culinary and domestic use for rolling pins, bowls, breadboards and so on. It is very easy to turn and takes a lovely finish straight off the tool.

Walnut

Walnut is smooth, lustrous, hard and strong. It ranges from light brown to nearly black in colour, with darker markings. The wood can have very attractive figuring and grain and it turns well. Really dark walnut is difficult to obtain, and the imported American walnut is much paler and less attractive.

Yew

Yew is a very dense softwood that ranges from orange to rich brown in colour with purplish tints and with a distinctive white sapwood. Because it has many knots, heart shakes and in-growing bark it can be a difficult timber to turn. However, all these faults can lead to a very attractive and decorative item.

IMPORTED WOODS

Ebony

The ideal ebony is jet black in colour but it may be found to have brown or grey stripes or mottling. The wood has a fine, even, texture and it is very dense. Ebony is used for knobs, keys for musical instruments and chessmen. It is imported, in relatively small sizes, from India and Sri Lanka.

Mahogany

There are many species of mahogany, but Brazilian mahogany, which is still available, is reddish-brown in colour with a medium weight and fairly fine texture. It has an even grain and turns very well. The timber can be stained to match older mahoganies. This wood is used for a whole range of turned items but check that it has come from a renewable resource before you buy it.

Pine

Pine comes in a wide variety of species that differ considerably in texture, colour and grain. Pine for DIY work needs to be selected with care if it is going to be turned. Pine from old items of furniture, such as church pews, can be extremely useful in restoration or repair turning. Pine can be stained to represent a wide number of other woods. Although pine turns well it is difficult to obtain crisp detail. It is most suitable for legs, feet, stair spindles and so on, but it is susceptible to worm damage and rot.

Materials other than Wood

Ivory, bone, tortoiseshell and horn may occasionally be required when repairing items. Clearly ivory is no longer available but artificial plastic versions of grained ivory are sold for turning and will give good results. Artificial bone and tortoiseshell are also now obtainable. Only small quantities of these materials are normally required for small knobs, chessmen or decorative trimmings. More detail is given in Chapter 13.

Rosewood

Rosewood varies in colour from dark brown to mauve red to a purplish-brown. The wood is hard, heavy and can be difficult to turn. It is used for high-quality turned items such as musical instruments.

Once it was abundant but is now not so readily available.

Exotic Woods
There are still plenty of exotic woods to buy but they are expensive and are usually only available in small quantities. Exotic timbers can be purchased from specialist turning suppliers.

WHERE TO BUY WOOD

SPECIALISTS

A very wide range of wood for spindle and faceplate turning is available from specialist turning suppliers. This may be an expensive way of purchasing timber but the wood will already be cut and seasoned, and it should have been carefully selected. It should therefore be free of faults, and for small items such as knobs, finials, and small feet, this can be a good source of supply.

RECLAIMED WOOD

Old, sound wood from furniture can be very useful if it is free from woodworm. It is always worth collecting any suitable old wood in case it comes in useful at a later date, but care needs to be taken to avoid injury from embedded nails and screws.

TIMBER MERCHANTS

Firms selling hardwoods and softwoods, both imported and local, usually advertise in local newspapers and in the telephone book. However, the quantities that such firms deal in will often be too large for the occasional repair task and some of the wood may well need to be seasoned. Reducing large planks of wood to a more manageable size can be difficult without the right equipment.

DIY STORES

Most DIY retailers stock planed-all-round softwood in reasonable sizes. The quality varies considerably, so great care needs to be taken when selecting wood from this source. Avoid pines that are obviously very resinous or too knotty.

OFF-CUTS

I purchase most of my home-grown woods from local joinery and carpentry firms as off-cuts. This is the cheapest way to buy wood, and with luck the firms will have something suitable.

WOODWORM

In a book about repair and restoration some words about woodworm infestation seem appropriate! Woodworm are actually beetles that live in wood and, unchecked, can completely destroy a piece of furniture. Woodworm attack is easily recognizable by the small, round flight holes on the surface of the wood. On furniture these are most likely to be found around joints and on the back or underside of the item. Whilst flight holes show that some of the beetles have emerged it is likely that larvae remain in the wood, damaging it further. Left untreated, there is a risk that infestation will spread to other items of furniture, floorboards and joists.

Proprietary woodworm killer solutions are available. When applied to bare wood the surfaces need to be given at least two coats, with particular attention given to end grain, corners and joints. In severe cases the liquid needs to be injected with a syringe into the flight holes and the treatment should be repeated. Liquid will not penetrate the polish on polished wood, so it is important to inject it into the flight holes at 2–2½in (5–6cm) intervals, and to flood

Fig. 37 Typical woodworm damage at the end of an oak leg where it has been in contact with the floor.

joints with the liquid before repeating the process. Take care to follow the instructions on the product exactly, and to wear suitable clothing and gloves. Any discarded wood should be removed and burnt.

ADHESIVES

Adhesives are an essential part of woodwork, used for attaching pieces of wood to each other and to other materials. There are many types available today, all with different properties, and advantages and disadvantages. The most common ones are discussed below.

PVA

This is a good, general-purpose woodworking glue sold under different names by all the major adhesive manufacturers. It is economical and has a long shelf life. The adhesive is non-toxic and it dries clear, giving a very strong bond; for best results leave the work cramped up overnight. Any excess glue oozing out of a joint should be wiped off immediately with a damp cloth before it stains the wood, otherwise it will be difficult to stain and polish. PVA is not a gap filler so the joint needs to be a good fit and the surfaces need to be clean and free of other adhesives.

HOT-MELT GLUE

I favour using a glue gun because it is quick and reliable. Sticks of adhesive come in a variety of different types for different materials. For wood a 30- to 100-second stick is most suitable, the sticks with a longer curing time giving more time to position the work. The glue sticks are used in an electric hot-melt glue gun, and after the initial investment in the gun this is

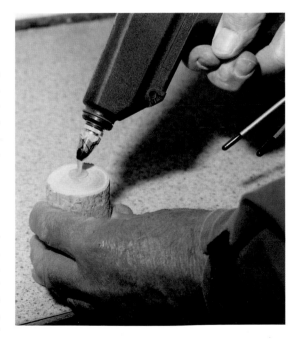

Fig. 38 A hot-melt glue gun.

an economical system. The glue has no unpleasant fumes and dries almost immediately. This makes it very useful for the turner when gluing wood blanks to a glue chuck. The glue is thick and allows even rough, unprepared wood to be glued. This system is particularly useful for gluing small pieces of expensive or exotic wood to a larger scrap piece of plywood or MDF to act as a holder whilst the wood is run through the bandsaw. In this way very little wastage occurs. It is also useful as an occasional, temporary measure to hold wood when drilling, and is very good for jig making.

SUPERGLUE

These are expensive glues with a relatively short shelf life. They do have a wide application in woodwork and give a very strong bond without the need to cramp. For the turner the glue is useful for glue chucking as it dries very quickly, but care is needed.

ANIMAL GLUE

This is the traditional adhesive for furniture joints and it is still used widely in restoration; it is particularly useful because it is gap filling. If restoration is necessary again at some point in the future it will be possible to part a joint with hot water or methylated spirit if this type of glue has been used. Animal glue is inexpensive; it comes in granules that are melted in a glue pot. This type of glue is slow to cure and the work does need cramping up.

CHAIR DOCTOR

This is a quite expensive modern adhesive that expands the wood, and is designed primarily to repair loose joints. It is good for spigots that are slightly too small, but both spigot and hole must be clean and free of old adhesives before application so that the wood can absorb the glue. It is clean to

> # Tips for Successful Gluing
>
> - Adhesive will not make a poor joint good!
> - Do not be impatient: allow plenty of time for the glue to cure
> - Always apply adhesive to a surface that is free of grease, polish, paint and old glue
> - Work in a well-ventilated workshop, as some adhesives have strong, unpleasant vapours
> - Take care to wipe away any glue that oozes out of a joint immediately
> - Use plenty of cramps to hold work firmly whilst curing takes place
> - Many adhesives are very volatile, and fire is always a hazard in a workshop
> - Store adhesives as instructed by the manufacturer

use, can be applied with a syringe to get the glue right into the hole, and is quick to cure. This is a particularly useful glue for anyone repairing or restoring chairs, as its name suggests!

EPOXY RESIN

Epoxy resin is a two-part adhesive, consisting of glue and a hardener, which are mixed together. This is not a very economical adhesive but it is gap filling, odourless and extremely useful where metal and wood are to be bonded. There is a fast version available, which cures in 5 minutes, as well as an alternative slow version, which cures in 24 hours.

— 6 —

Finishing

Turning is a fast way of achieving results but finishing takes time and lots of patience, and is often a stage that is rushed through too quickly, resulting in good work being spoiled. Good finishing should enhance the wood to show the colour and grain to their best advantage and give durable, long-lasting protection with a pleasant, smooth, silky feel to the wood. It is very difficult to match the colour and patina of a newly turned item to the host item. For really old or valuable pieces of furniture it is recommended that the turner has the work stained and finished professionally. It takes many, many years to become a really competent finisher and the woodworker cannot expect to be an expert at everything! If, on the other hand, the item is of little monetary value then it is worth having a go – it is only with practice that skills improve.

The main problem that the finisher will encounter is making a smart, newly turned item blend in and not look like an obvious replacement. This applies particularly to furniture and sometimes it might be practical to repolish the whole piece. Alternatively, it may be possible to distress the new item, but this is an art in itself! It will usually be easier to finish the new part off the lathe so that it can be matched, but one-off items, such as handles, can be finished in the lathe.

SANDING

HAND-HELD ABRASIVE

If sharp, well-honed tools, good holding devices and correct technique have been used in turning the item, very little sanding should be necessary. There are plenty of abrasives to choose from, and turners will probably have their own favourites. For the pieces featured in this book I have used a cloth-backed, flexible, aluminium oxide abrasive in a range of grits from 180 to 400. This abrasive is very effective for general sanding on the lathe and its flexibility means it can get into tight curves and contours without cracking. The cloth back

Fig. 39 Hold the abrasive under the spindle. An extraction hose held close to the work will take away a good deal of the dust. Note that the toolrest and holder have both been moved completely out of the way.

47

makes the abrasive comfortable to use, and it can even be washed out when it becomes clogged with dust and reused time and again. The abrasive comes on a roll in various widths, and although it seems expensive at the time of purchase, it proves economical in the long run.

POWERED SANDERS

Small sanding discs, which fit on to a plate with an arbor to use with an electric drill or a flexible drive, can be useful if you have a large area to sand. The discs come in a wide range of grits and are held on the plate

Fig. 40 To sand large areas, a grip-a-disc system used with an electric drill is useful. The Velcro foam-mounted abrasive provides a pliable sanding system. It is used with the lathe running, and the result is virtually line-free. This is a very dusty system, so a mask and extractor are needed.

Fig. 41 Using the non-powered sanding system to sand a large foot.

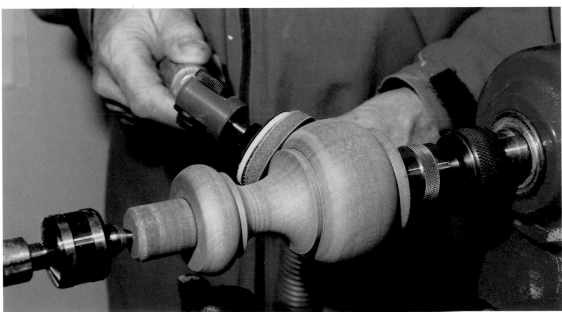

Fig. 42 A non-woven web product is excellent for burnishing.

with Velcro. This method of sanding is noisy and dusty but it is very quick and effective; however, a dust mask is essential!

NON-POWERED SANDERS

The hand-held, non-powered sander has similar Velcro discs to the powered sander, but it does not produce so much dust and is easy to use. As with the powered version, there is minimal risk of lines forming on the work during sanding.

HAND SANDING OFF THE LATHE

Sometimes it is necessary to hand finish a piece off the lathe, and for this a fine, foam-backed, aluminium oxide abrasive is particularly comfortable to use.

BURNISHING AND DENIBBING

For final burnishing or denibbing, or for applying a wax or oil finish, a non-woven nylon web material is excellent. Such a product consists of fibres on which aluminium oxide or silicon carbide grains are firmly bonded by resin. As the grain is used up, fresh grain becomes exposed deeper in the mesh. The large spaces

Tips for Successful Sanding

- Sanding produces harmful wood dust and every precaution should be taken by the turner not to inhale the dust. Always wear an approved disposable dust mask, respirator or air-flow helmet, and use an extraction system wherever possible. To be effective, disposable dust masks should have the European Standard EN 149 FFP1 OR 2 stamped on them. Unmarked 'nuisance' masks are not suitable. Holding the extraction hose as near to the sanding action as possible helps to reduce the amount of dust in the atmosphere

- When sanding or polishing in the lathe, remove the toolrest and move the tool holder out of the way. Hold the abrasive underneath the work

- When sanding work mounted on a faceplate, such as the inside of a bowl, hold the abrasive between 8 and 7 o'clock with the fingers pointing downwards

- Keep the abrasive moving all the time from side to side to avoid forming lines on the work.

- The grit number refers to the number of grain particles per unit area – the higher the number, the finer the grit. Work from coarse grit (180) through to fine grit (400)

- Do not over-sand and take away the crisp edges that have been formed within the web allow dust particles to circulate freely, thus preventing clogging. The result is a long-lasting, very flexible, non-clogging material, which can get into nooks and crannies with ease. There is no build-up of heat and the material can be rinsed out under running water to remove dust. It is sold in hand pads of 280 grit fine, 360 grit very fine and 1500 grit ultra fine. This product can be used instead of steel wool and is far superior. There are no metal fibres left embedded in the wood grain or in the polish tin after use, and no risk of fine cuts to the fingers.

Wood can also be burnished by gently rubbing wood shavings on the rotating work. This is a natural polishing process.

STAINING

There are many stains available on the market, and they break down basically into spirit stains, water stains and the relatively modern acrylic stains. I favour spirit stains because they penetrate quite deeply into the wood and are relatively easy to apply, but they do give off strong vapours and so must be applied in a well-ventilated area. Water-based stains tend to raise the grain of the wood.

Proprietary spirit stains are available in a wide range of colours, which can be inter-mixed or laid over one another. Each colour will not necessarily transform a piece of wood into the wood named on the tin; for example, Antique Pine applied on to new pine may not come out quite as you wish and some experimentation is strongly recommended on scraps of wood similar to the wood being turned.

APPLYING STAIN

The surface to be stained should be free from glue residue and greasy finger marks, or an uneven, patchy finish will result.

Spirit stains are applied to the bare, sanded wood with a brush; the surplus should be removed with a cloth straight away. The brush can be cleaned in white spirit. A second coat can be applied within the hour but after this it is advisable to leave the work for 24 hours between subsequent applications and to allow the wood to dry thoroughly before any polishing is attempted. Patience is really necessary when it comes to finishing!

Work from a lighter colour to a darker colour rather than the other way round. Do not be afraid to use one colour over another to achieve the shade you are looking for. Denib lightly between each application with a very fine abrasive. Always work in a well-ventilated area and wear disposable gloves. Finally, remember that these stains are not a finish in themselves: they are purely a method of colouring the wood, and if the wood is left at this stage without further finishing, the stain will begin to fade.

SEALING AND POLISHING

The following finishes can be used on bare, sanded wood or over stained wood to finally seal and polish the work.

CELLULOSE SANDING SEALER

Sanding sealer is a very quick-drying product for turned items, which, if carefully rubbed down between coats, will produce a durable, high-gloss finish. It is applied with a soft brush, which needs to be cleaned in cellulose thinners. This finish can be difficult to use on a large item because it dries so quickly, making it difficult to produce an even finish, but for smaller items it works well. The major disadvantage of cellulose sanding sealer is that it gives off very strong fumes, so it must be used in a well-ventilated area!

Fig. 43 Applying spirit wood stain with a brush.

If the sealer is applied with the work stationary but still on the lathe, denibbing between coats is made much easier, but do protect the lathe bars. If applied with the wood rotating the cellulose will spray everywhere and prove very difficult to remove. Apply a coat of sanding sealer with a brush and leave it to dry for 24 hours. After gently denibbing with fine abrasive, apply a second coat and again leave to dry. This can be repeated if necessary. Finally, wax the wood with furniture polish.

VARNISH

Clear polyurethane varnish is available in matt, satin and gloss finishes. The varnish should be applied following the manufacturer's instructions, and several coats of varnish can be built up. Gently denib with fine abrasive between coats and leave plenty of time for each application to dry. Finally polish with wax furniture polish to give a very good, durable finish. A word of caution: universal coloured varnishes are not really suitable for the type of work described in this book.

FRENCH POLISH

This is the traditional method of polishing. It is a lengthy and skilful process, but kits are now available to make it easier. French polishing leaves a high-gloss surface.

FINISHING OILS

Finishing oils are a blend of high-quality oils, resins and dryers, which are resistant to water, alcohol and food acids. They are safe and easy to apply without any unpleasant fumes. Apply the oil with a soft brush and allow 15 minutes for it to penetrate the wood before wiping off any excess with a clean cloth. New wood will require two or three coats, but always allow 3–5 hours drying time between coats. Additional coats can be applied any time thereafter as required to freshen up the wood. Oil gives a natural lustre.

FRICTION POLISH

This type of polish is applied with kitchen paper or a rag to the wood while it is turning in the lathe, and it seals and polishes in one operation, giving a high shine. The polished surface is built up by the increase in pressure. The product is flammable and should only be used in a well-ventilated area. Two shades are available: white and dark. The white is the most useful and is used on pale timbers, while the darker shade is intended for darker woods. Friction polish is very quick and easy to use but of course it is only suitable for turned items where the wood can stay on the lathe and does not need to be matched to a host item. This makes it particularly suitable for items such as one-off handles, for example.

CARNAUBA WAX

This is a sold in solid stick form. The carnauba wax is blended with other substances to soften it slightly and improve the flow qualities, because carnauba itself is very hard and would scratch the workpiece. The wax can be used on bare wood, or over sanding sealer or friction polish. When buffed, it produces a warm glow with a hard, lasting finish. Apply the wax directly to the revolving wood and build up a high polish by applying pressure with a cloth.

BUFFING

Woods such as boxwood, and materials such as alternative ivory can be polished to a very high finish on a buffing wheel using a polishing compound.

Fig. 44 Carnauba wax is applied directly to the revolving wood.

Fig. 45 *Buffing boxwood with car polish on a cotton mop.*

Fig. 46 *A black stain finish can be painted directly on to boxwood.*

PAINTING

Sometimes the turned replacement will need to be painted instead of being stained. After sanding the wood smooth, apply an acrylic primer; when this is dry, sand back to the wood to achieve a good, smooth surface to paint on.

METALLIC FINISH

Gold, silver, bronze, and pewter metallic finishes are available in a liquid paint, in paste form or in spray cans. None are a substitute for gold or silver leaf, but true gilding is again a very skilled technique. However, very credible results can be

Fig. 47 Applying liquid gold to a finial directly on to the wood.

achieved with these metallic finishes and they are easy to apply, so well worth trying. Buy them in art shops. You are unlikely to need to finish a very large item; an example could well be a clock finial, a decorative ball in a mirror frame or some turned half or quarter moulding.

Tips for Successful Finishing

- You will need lots of patience!
- Do not apply a wax finish on a spigot that is to be glued into a hole
- Always make sure that all excess glue is wiped from the surface of wood before it dries, otherwise the stain will be unable to penetrate, and an uneven, patchy finish will result
- Apply varnish in a dust-free atmosphere
- Use a yacht varnish if the turning is to be exposed to the weather
- Always work in a well-ventilated area when applying finishes, as many emit strong, unpleasant vapours
- Take care where you store your finishes, as many are highly inflammable
- Rubbing a hand over the rotating work is not good practice, as grease from the fingers will inhibit the even penetration of stains or polishes

7

PLANNING

When contemplating undertaking a new restoration job, I suggest you ask yourself the following questions before even picking up a pencil:

- Have I sufficient skill to undertake this task?
- Have I a lathe and equipment that is suitable?
- What are the dimensions, measurements and shapes involved?
- What type of wood am I going to use and how am I going to hold it securely on the lathe?
- Where am I going to make my initial cuts and how am I going to develop the shapes?
- How am I going to finish the item?
- How am I going to fix the replacement on to host item?

USEFUL EQUIPMENT FOR THE PLANNING STAGE

VERNIER CALLIPERS

These callipers are used mainly by engineers but they are particularly useful for taking off measurements from turned items. They are graduated in imperial and metric measurements, and are very accurate inside, outside and in depth. Some Vernier callipers have a dial gauge, which makes them easier to read; the really expensive models even have a digital read-out. This instrument is usually made in high-quality stainless steel, but high-impact plastic versions are also produced. There is a slight risk that the measuring surfaces on the plastic callipers may become damaged if the instrument is – inadvertently

Fig. 48 Using Vernier callipers to measure the diameter of a cove.

and incorrectly – used on rotating wood in the lathe. The wood should not be rotating when measurements are being taken because there is always a risk that the callipers will catch on the wood and be swung round to injure the turner.

PROFILE GAUGE

This measuring instrument consists of metal or plastic pins arranged in a holder rather like a comb. When the gauge is pressed against a curved item the pins take the shape of that form, and this can then be drawn around as a template with reasonable accuracy. The gauges with plastic pins are more appropriate for wooden items since they do not mark the surface of the wood.

COMPASSES AND DIVIDERS

A good pair each of these drawing instruments will last a lifetime.

Fig. 49 *Taking off the shape of a newel post top with a profile gauge.*

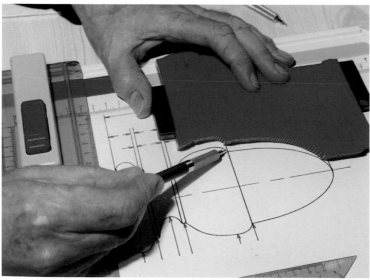

Fig. 50 *Drawing round the gauge to transfer the shape to card.*

Fig. 51 An A3 drawing board and useful drawing equipment.

DRAWING BOARD

A lightweight A3 plastic drawing board with sliding scale and square is more than adequate. A board such as this is easy to store when not in use, it holds the paper securely and can even be used on the knee.

PENCILS AND PENS

Clutch pencils with very fine leads, a good soft rubber and fine felt pens will be all that is required.

MEASUREMENTS – METRIC VERSUS IMPERIAL

It is always difficult to convert imperial to metric and vice versa to give good, round numbers. Some materials are sold in imperial thicknesses and some in metric, and this also applies to tools such as drills and turning chisels. In most people's toolboxes there will be imperially calibrated drills, for example, mixed together with metric accessories. In repair and restoration work the majority of items will be in imperial.

The conversions are often rounded off and are not precise, so the woodworker needs to take particular care that the actual measurement is used when planning and marking out work. I have tried to get the conversions in this book as accurate as possible but it is well worth double-checking before producing an item.

STARTING TO PLAN

It is wise to spend time assessing and planning a particular repair task, and research may have to be undertaken before starting work. It is advisable to sit down with paper and pencil and think the whole exercise through. Where the turner has an existing example of the piece to be replaced it is relatively easy to analyse the item and to make a detailed drawing. For example, you may have a table with one table leg damaged but three sound legs. You have more of a problem when there is only one turned item and it is missing! An example would perhaps be a single finial on a piece of furniture. To get some ideas, research will be needed and books, antique guides and visits to old houses, shops, museums and churches can all be helpful.

The final drawing should aim to give the turner dimensions, diameters and the positions of lines where a new shape starts, so that the turning can develop in stages until the final form, with the correct proportions and diameters, is achieved. Throughout the book there are examples of drawings and turning plans. You may consider all this preparation unnecessary but I have found from experience that you will end up with very disappointing results and will waste time and wood unnecessarily if you omit the planning stage.

MAKING A TEMPLATE OR TURNING GUIDE

The following example shows the stages from planning through to turning to make an acorn newel post top. If the same principle is applied to other forms, and the

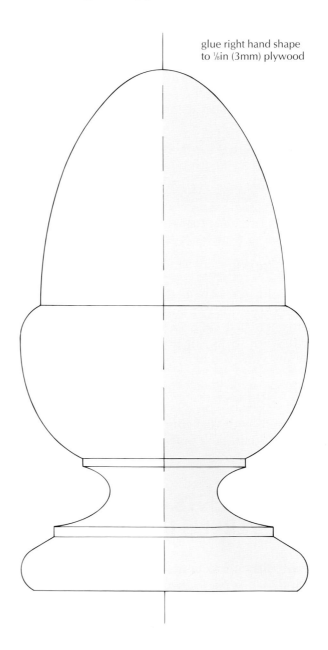

glue right hand shape
to ⅛in (3mm) plywood

Fig. 52 An accurate drawing.

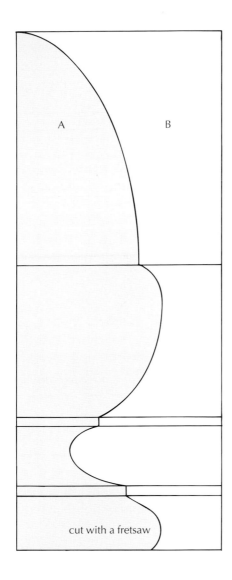

cut with a fretsaw

sequence is followed, any shape can be produced accurately and repeated as many times as necessary with identical results.

1. Make an accurate, full-sized drawing from the original using a profile gauge to copy shapes, and callipers to take off measurements.
2. Cut the drawing down the centre-line to give two symmetrical halves.
3. Glue the right-hand half on to a piece of ⅛in (3mm) birch plywood or MDF.
4. Cut round the plywood with a fretsaw to produce guide A and template B.
5. Mark the diameter of the slots on guide A. In the example, two slots show the two fillets and the third slot gives the area at the top edge of the cup.

HOW TO USE THE TEMPLATE AND GUIDE

1. Turn a prepared blank to the maximum diameter.

(Left) *Fig. 53 Guide and template.*

(Below) *Fig. 54 Completed guide and template.*

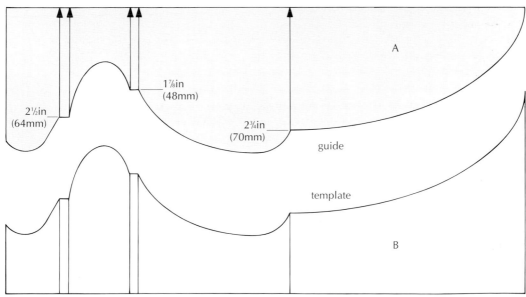

A

2½in
(64mm)

1⅞in
(48mm)

2¾in
(70mm)

guide

template

B

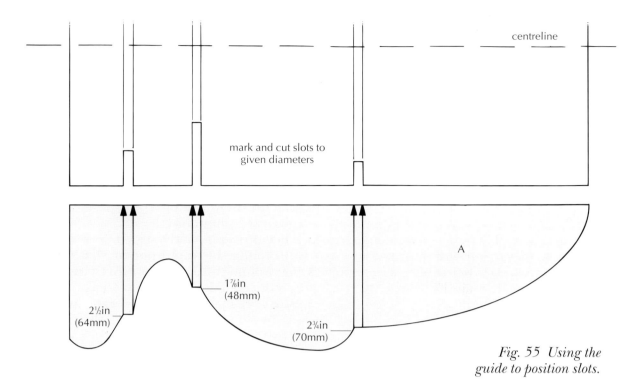

mark and cut slots to
given diameters

2½in
(64mm)

1⅞in
(48mm)

2¾in
(70mm)

centreline

A

*Fig. 55 Using the
guide to position slots.*

2. Using guide A, mark the position of the three slots.
3. Cut the slots with a ⅛in (3mm) parting tool to just above the required diameters noted on guide A.

4. Commence shaping the acorn, cup, cove and base, and use template B to check the correct development of the planned shape.
5. Crisp up the fillets with a skew chisel.
6. Sand, burnish, stain or polish as required.

Fig. 56 Using the template to check form.

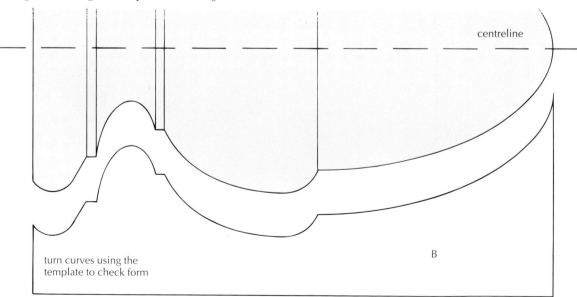

centreline

turn curves using the
template to check form

B

8

HANDLES AND KNOBS

HANDLES

Looking through a reprint of a Victorian catalogue I found turned wooden handles on all manner of weird and wonderful bygones, with the majority to be found on domestic and gardening equipment, from rolling pins and coffee pots to hearth brushes, wheelbarrows and scythes! Hard daily domestic use, rot and woodworm take their toll on handles of old implements and many have long gone or are damaged. The collectors of these bygones wishing to replace missing or broken handles should take care to produce a handle that is of the correct shape and of the same wood if possible. However, on a more everyday item, which has no intrinsic value and is in current use, a good, strong, well-shaped handle will probably be all that is needed.

FIXING

When planning how you are going to replace a handle, consideration has to be given to the way in which it is fixed to the tool or item. For

Fig. 57 A collection of handles.

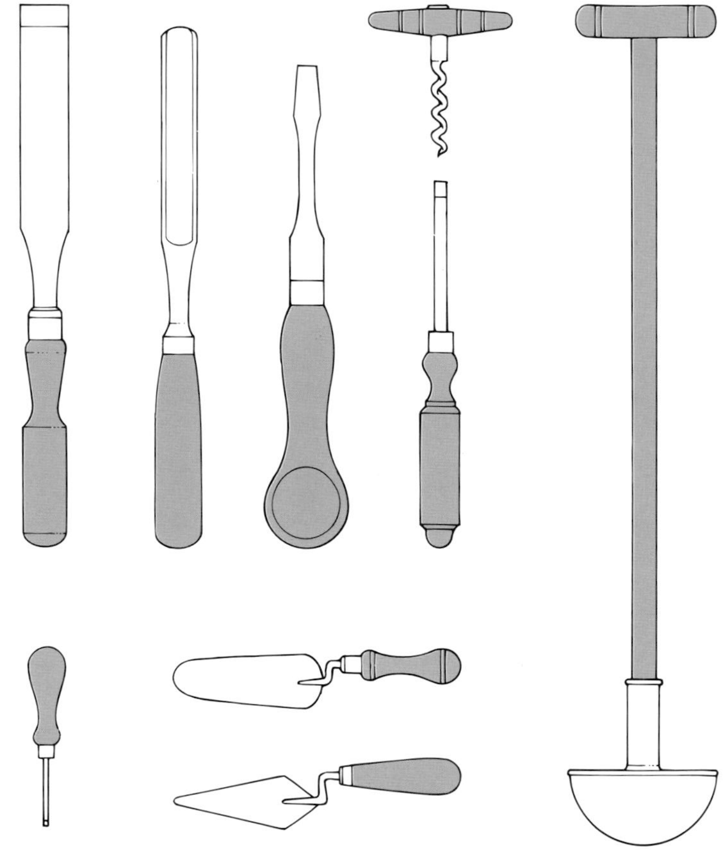

Fig. 58 Some examples of handle shapes.

(Below) Fig. 59 Shapes of tangs.

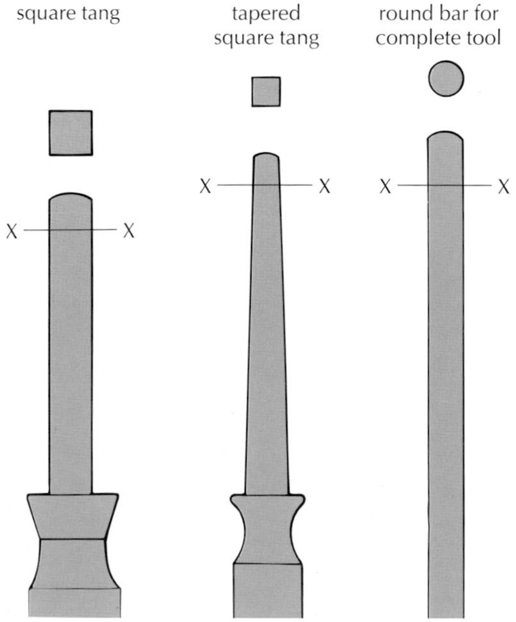

square tang

tapered square tang

round bar for complete tool

example, some turning chisels are made from round machined stock so they have a round tang, while forged tools usually have a square, rectangular or tapered tang where the red-hot steel has been hammered by hand or machine to shape, and on early tools this tang is often quite rough and uneven. Tools such as woodworking chisels, files and garden implements fall into this latter group.

The purpose of handles on both types of tanged tools is to give the operator something to grip on to and to give protection to the palm of the hand. Another group of handles comprises those designed to rotate on a shank or axle, and these are found on winding handles, brace and bits, mincers, old-fashioned mangles and so on. Then there are the handles that are tapered to push fit into a

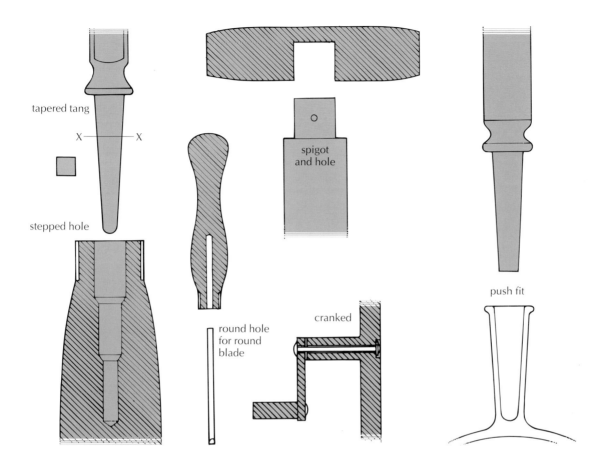

Fig. 60 Methods of fixing handles.

socket, such as those on a warming pan, and finally others with a spigot to match a drilled hole, a common method for attaching handles to a brush or garden implement.

FERRULES

A ferrule is a brass ring fitted on a tool handle to reduce the risk of the wood splitting when the tang of the tool is inserted into the handle. As the tang is forced down into the pre-drilled hole the wood is pushed out against the brass band making a tight, secure fit. Ferrules are traditionally made of brass, but some are chrome plated. They

are readily available from specialist suppliers in various sizes and lengths, but sometimes it is necessary to cut brass tube, of a suitable diameter, for a handle of an unusual size.

SHAPE AND DESIGN

Handles are functional and need to be designed to be suitable for their task. It is important that they are the right length and circumference, strong and smooth, and shaped to fit comfortably in the hand. If the original handle is still discernible, then the task is to copy it and find suitable wood for a good match. If the handle has gone completely then it is usually not too difficult to find similar examples in books, magazines and old catalogues, and then to choose a suitable design.

A NEW HANDLE FOR A TURNING TOOL

The method described below will create a handle suitable for a turning tool, woodworking chisel, screwdriver or a gardening implement; the length and diameter can be adapted as required. Beech, ash, sycamore, boxwood and rosewood are all suitable woods for tool handles. The lathe produces a round handle in section but it is feasible to plane, or sand, a flat on one or more sides of the handle to increase grip or the stability of the tool on a bench. Alternatively the blank can be planed to give a multi-faceted surface before it is put in the lathe, and the centre section left unturned. Accurate drilling for the centre hole to take the tang

is very important and detailed instructions on how to do this are given in Chapter 4.

Method Using a Ring Centre
1. Prepare a blank of suitable wood, long enough to produce a handle of the required length, plus ¾in (18mm) of waste wood, and thick enough to produce the maximum diameter required for the handle. Fit a ring centre into the headstock and a revolving centre into the tailstock and set the lathe speed to 2,000rpm.
2. Mark the centre of each end of the spindle and centre pop with a punch and mount the spindle between centres. Tighten up the tailstock so that sufficient friction is produced to drive the spindle. Additional tailstock pressure may be needed during the turning process.
3. Position the toolrest so that the top edge is just below the centre-line and there is no more than ¼in (6mm) between the

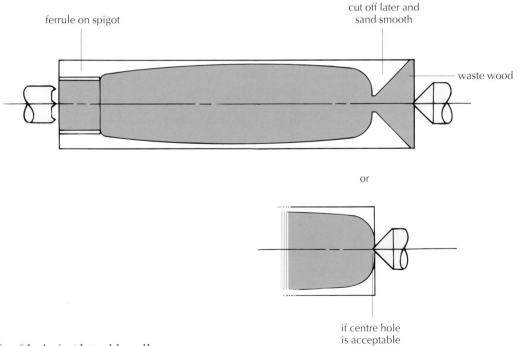

cut off later and sand smooth

ferrule on spigot

waste wood

or

if centre hole is acceptable

Fig. 61 A simple tool handle.

edges of the blank and the top of the rest. Rotate the wood by hand to ensure that there are no obstructions.

4. Using the roughing-out gouge, turn the blank to the round to a diameter just above the maximum required, and then mark the length of the spigot in pencil at the headstock end and set a pair of Vernier callipers to match the inside diameter of the selected ferrule.

5. Using a parting tool start turning the spigot. The ferrule should be a good fit and not loose. One of the advantages of using the ring centre is that the wood can be removed and remounted accurately, with confidence, after checking to see if the ferrule fits. It may be possible to place a ferrule over the body of the ring centre so that the spindle does not need to be removed for checking.

Fig. 62 Turning the blank to the round with a roughing-out gouge.

Fig. 63 Cutting the spigot with a parting tool. Note the ferrule on the body of the ring centre, ready to be slipped on to the spigot.

6. Once the ferrule is in position on the spigot, cover it over with some masking tape in case it becomes damaged by a tool or scratched with abrasive, and turn the handle to shape with a spindle gouge, a skew or both. Partially form the handle at the tailstock end, leaving about ⅜in (10mm) diameter waste wood to be cut off by hand later. Alternatively, if you do not mind the centre pop at the end of the handle, the work can be shaped with the skew right down to the revolving centre point. Decorative shallow V cuts can be made with the long point of the skew and these cuts can provide some extra grip.

7. Remove the toolrest, and sand, burnish and polish the handle. Drill the centre hole for the tang either in the lathe or in a bench drill. Place epoxy resin into the drilled hole and tap the tool blade

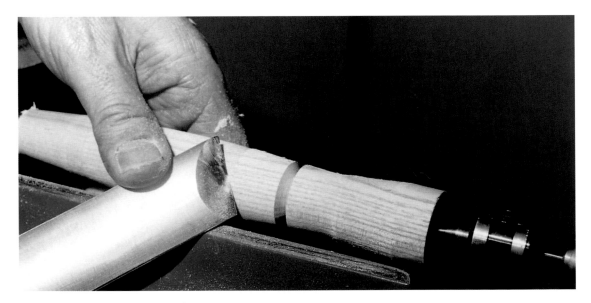

Fig. 64 Partially form the handle at the tailstock end with the skew.

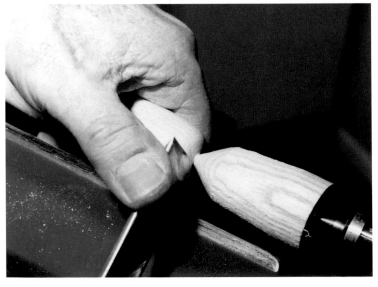

Fig. 65 Leave some waste wood to be cut off by hand later.

into position. If the tang is rectangular it can still go into a round hole. The edges of the tang will wedge quite satisfactorily as the blade is pushed down into the wood and the epoxy resin will fill any gaps.

Method Using a Friction Drive

The stepped friction drive offers an alternative way of driving a spindle when making handles. It has steps of ⅛, ¼, ⅜ and ⅝in (3, 6, 10 and 16mm) diameter. The blank can be pre-drilled before it goes on the

Fig. 66 A blank mounted on the friction drive with the ferrule over the drive. The blank has been pre-drilled with a ¼in (6mm) hole.

Fig. 67 Cutting the spigot with a parting tool and checking to see that the ferrule is a good fit.

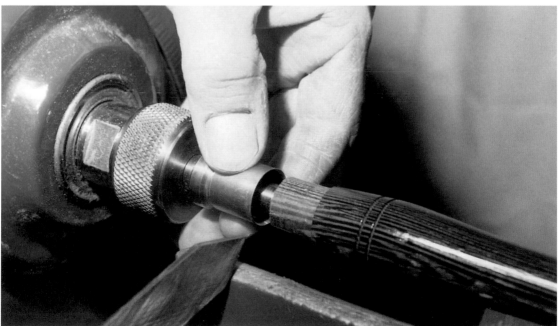

Fig. 68 Polishing the rosewood handle with friction polish. Take care not to polish the spigot!

Fig. 69 The stepped friction drive shown with a ¼in (6mm) spindle gouge fitted in the completed rosewood tool handle.

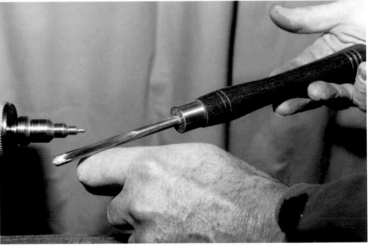

lathe and this is a particularly good option for round-shanked tools that match these diameters. If the shank of the tool is of a different diameter it is an easy matter to redrill the hole to the correct size when work on the handle has been completed. The pre-drilled hole will act as a guide for the larger drill bit, ensuring that the enlarged hole is absolutely true and accurate. Because a friction drive and a revolving centre are used for this method it will be necessary to increase the tailstock pressure at intervals during turning if the spindle should start to slip.

A NEW HANDLE FOR A BRACE AND BIT

Woodworking tool handles take quite a battering over the years. We have looked at replacement handles for chisels, files and screwdrivers, but other tools, such as a brace and bit, may have a damaged rotating crank handle or a breast handle that needs replacing.

Method

1. To turn the crank handle, prepare a blank to match the size of the old handle in a suitable wood. Drill the blank throughout its length with a ⅝in (16mm) Forstner bit in a bench drill. Mount one end on a stepped friction drive on the ⅝in (16mm) step in the headstock and support the other end with a revolving centre in the tailstock. Turn the handle with a roughing out gouge and finish off with a skew chisel to form a sausage shape with square ends.

2. Fitting can be a problem because often the brace cannot be disassembled as the steel shank is made in one piece. The solution is to cut the handle down the centre and then to glue the two halves back together on each side of the crank using an epoxy resin. Cutting a relatively small handle accurately in half can be made much easier by turning up a spigot on the end of a square piece of scrap stock to match the diameter of the hole in the handle. The work is then pushed onto the spigot and the jig passed through the bandsaw with the rectangular side of the jig against the fence. When drilling the hole in the handle it is important to make sure that an allowance is made for the fact that the blank is going to be cut in half and that the handle needs to rotate freely on the crank.

3. The next task is to replace the breast handle. This handle is domed in shape and is screwed on to a flange that rotates in a bearing. Mount a suitable blank in

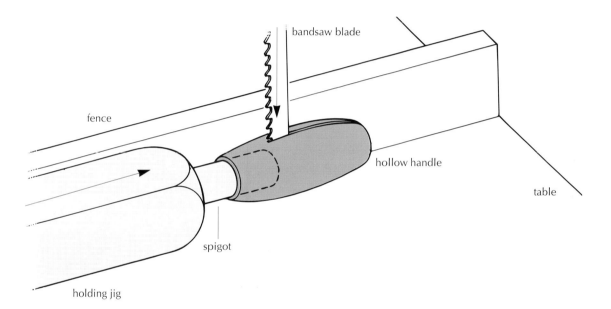

(Above) *Fig. 70 Cutting the handle for the brace on the bandsaw.*

Fig. 71 Checking the brace against the work to make sure that the recesses are a good fit.

a screw chuck and turn to the round. Face off the end with a spindle gouge and cut a recess to match the depth and diameter of the flange. Cut a further recess in the centre to take the rear part of the bearings and the locking nut.

4. At this stage check the brace against the work in the lathe to make sure that the recesses are a good fit and that there is nothing to impede rotation. Then partially shape the underside of the handle with a spindle gouge and part off.

5. Make a jam chuck with the remaining wood on the screw chuck to hold the reversed, partially turned handle in a good, tight fit so that the front of the work can be turned, sanded and polished. With the work removed from the

Fig. 72 A jam chuck holds the reversed, partially turned handle.

Fig. 73 The brace and bit showing the new breast handle and the crank handle about to be glued together on each side of the shaft.

lathe it is a simple matter to drill pilot holes for the screws and to fit the new handle on to the flange.

WINDING HANDLES

There are many types of winding handle, from the kitchen mincer, the old-fashioned mangle and the wind-up gramophone right through to clock-winding handles, but they all share the principle of a handle rotating on a metal shaft. Clock-winding handles belonging to old long-case clocks are particularly interesting, and, because they are constantly in use, they do suffer over the years. The handle should not be too big, but must be big enough to make the winding

handle clearly visible, as they have a habit of getting lost! Enough of the original handle may remain to give an idea of shape and size; the handles were commonly made from boxwood or fruit wood.

Method
1. Drill a small blank of boxwood through its centre and mount it on a stepped friction drive in the headstock, and support the tailstock end with a revolving centre.
2. Turn the blank to the round with a roughing-out gouge and shape with a spindle gouge. Detail can be added with a spindle gouge and a small skew.
3. Sand and polish the handle to give a smooth finish.

(Above) *Fig. 74 Some examples of clock-winding handles.*

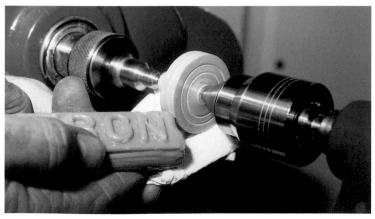

Fig. 75 Applying carnauba wax to a boxwood clock handle.

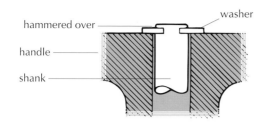

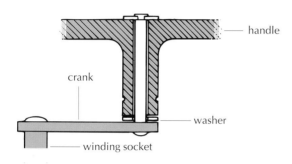

Fig. 76 Clock-winding handles.

4. When it comes to fitting the handle, a little work is often necessary with a reamer and file because shanks are often of an irregular diameter, and it is important that the handle should rotate freely. The handle is usually held in place with a washer, and again a little metalwork may be needed to burr over the end of the shaft to hold the washer in position. It is a good idea to put any spare nuts and washers that come your way into an odd box – they always come in handy at some stage!

WARMING PAN HANDLES

The copper warming pan was once in constant daily use; today it is usually only seen as an ornament hanging on the wall. The handle on a pan may not be original; some are well shaped in fruit wood with a patina acquired over the years, while others are very

basic and quite crude. It is not unusual to find a pan handle riddled with woodworm and often it is suspiciously short where the damaged wood has been cut off. The photograph shows a well-shaped handle that has been shortened at some stage, and is now a poor fit. Before making a new handle it is worth looking at a number of similar warming pans in books and antique shops.

If you have a lathe with a long enough bed you will be able to turn the handle in one piece. If this is not possible, however, do not despair! I will explain how to turn the handle in two separate lengths with a spigot and a hole to join them together. Although I have described making a handle for a warming pan the same principle applies to any long handle (*see* Fig. 77).

Oval Handles

Some tool handles, and the majority of knife handles, are oval in section rather than round. To make a new oval handle it will be necessary to use an off-centre chuck. There are several different types on the market, each working on a different principle, but they all come with detailed instructions. Some of these chucks offer a facility to turn hexagonal and other multi-faceted spindles, and they can also be used to produce cranks, which would be of use in restoring an automaton.

A Long Handle Turned in One Length
1. Make a turning guide with the appropriate datum lines clearly marked.
2. Cut a blank 1½ × 1½ × 32in (38 × 38 × 813mm); woods such as mahogany, yew, beech and fruit wood are all suitable. It is important that care is taken to square off the ends of the blank so that they are

absolutely true. Sand the ends on a disc sander if possible. Centre mark each end and centre pop.

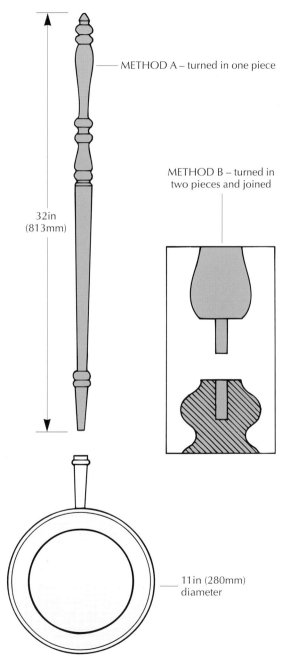

Fig. 77 *A warming-pan handle.*

METHOD A – turned in one piece

METHOD B – turned in two pieces and joined

32in (813mm)

11in (280mm) diameter

3. Mount the blank in the lathe with a ring centre in the headstock and a revolving centre in the tailstock. Set the lathe speed to 2,000rpm and turn the blank to the round with a roughing-out gouge.

4. Mark the datum lines with a pencil on the revolving wood, using the prepared turning guide to show where the initial cuts are to be made, and start shaping the handle using a spindle gouge and a skew. Because this is a long spindle the turner will experience a degree of whip in the middle. Steady the wood with the hand or with a lathe steady designed for the purpose. If the wood is not steadied the surface will show ribbing caused by the tool bouncing on the vibrating wood.

5. After turning the spindle to the required shape remove the toolrest and sand and burnish the work. The handle can be stained and finished on or off the lathe.

A Long Handle Turned in Two Parts

1. Make a turning guide and decide where the most inconspicuous place will be to make the join.

2. Prepare a blank 1½ × 1½ × 33in (38 × 38 × 838mm) and cut it into two pieces. Blank A will have a hole drilled in one end and blank B will have an extra length allowance of 1in (25mm) for a spigot. It is important that care is taken to square off the ends of each blank so that they are absolutely true.

3. Mark and centre pop the centre of blank A and drill it in a bench drill to produce a hole to match the diameter of the pin in a hollow ring centre; this is usually ⁵⁄₁₆in (8mm).

4. Push the drilled blank firmly on to the pin until the ring is in contact with the end face of the wood. Bring up the tailstock fitted with a revolving centre for support and turn the wood to shape. Remove the toolrest, sand and burnish the work and then remove it from the lathe.

Fig. 78 Pushing the drilled blank firmly on to the pin on the hollow ring centre.

Fig. 79 Cutting a spigot with a parting tool. Note the flat area, ready to take the glue.

5. Mount blank B between centres with a conventional ring centre in the headstock and a revolving centre in the tailstock, and turn to shape. Remove the toolrest, and sand and burnish the work.

6. Replace the toolrest and cut an ⁵⁄₁₆in (8mm) diameter spigot 1in (25mm) long at the tailstock end. Do not do this before turning is completed because the slightest catch could well break the spigot.

7. The area surrounding the spigot and hole should have a matching flat of about ¼in (6mm), so that when the spigot is inserted into the hole and the two parts are glued together there is sufficient area to give a really stable and strong joint. Line up the grain as well as possible before the glue cures. Stain and finish the handle off the lathe.

Fig. 80 The two parts ready for gluing. Line up the grain as well as possible.

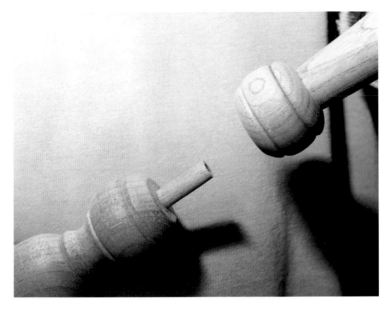

Fig. 81 The new handle ready to push-fit into the warming pan's tapered copper socket; the original shortened handle was a poor fit. The handle is held in place with a copper rivet.

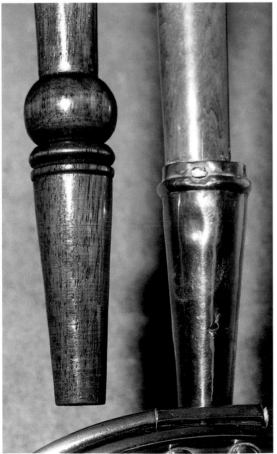

KNOBS

Knobs are particularly susceptible to damage and replacements are often needed. The wood in old furniture becomes brittle over the years when kept in a centrally heated environment, and it is not unusual to find that a knob is completely missing or is partly damaged.

Wooden knobs were dear to Victorian hearts and were frequently used as a replacement for brass drop handles on chests of drawers of earlier periods in order to bring them 'up to date' in line with the current fashion. This led to the ruin of many fine eighteenth-century pieces! Knobs are most commonly found on items of pine furniture such as chests of drawers, wardrobes, cupboards and kitchen table drawers. It is unlikely that all the knobs on a piece of furniture will be lost, so there will usually be an example to use as a pattern for the replacement. Sometimes, on an antique piece for example, it will be possible to splice a new piece of wood on to the damaged knob and then to turn it; in this way as much of the original wood is preserved as

Fig. 82 A selection of old and damaged knobs all needing attention!

possible. You may also decide to replace all the knobs on a particular piece of furniture because you dislike them!

Knob Shape

A well-shaped knob should be tactile with no sharp edges, and the fingers should slip comfortably between the base flange and the domed head.

A knob on a drawer that is constantly opened and shut takes considerable strain and often fails because of the way it is fixed to the carcass, so the method of fixing is an important consideration at the planning stage.

A TYPICAL VICTORIAN KNOB WITH A PLAIN SPIGOT

There are a number of ways to turn a knob and the following example is one simple method using a screw chuck. The drawing for this knob is taken from a Victorian oak

knob that I cut in half in order to produce a template. It has a typical dome shape and was once part of a chest of drawers. A knob like this would have been made from pine, beech, mahogany, elm, walnut, oak or a similar wood to match the carcass. Contemporary country-style furniture is usually made in pine and plain wooden knobs are commonly mass-produced.

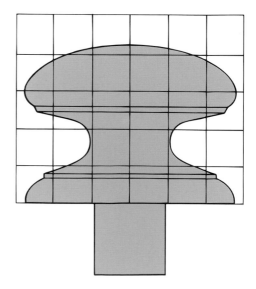

Fig. 83 A plan for a knob for a chest of drawers.

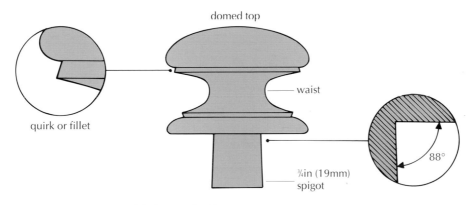

domed top

waist

quirk or fillet

88°

¾in (19mm)
spigot

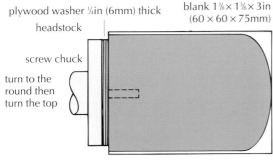

plywood washer ¼in (6mm) thick

headstock

screw chuck

turn to the
round then
turn the top

blank 1⅜ × 1⅜ × 3in
(60 × 60 × 75mm)

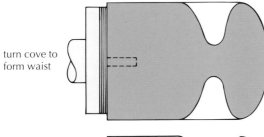

turn cove to
form waist

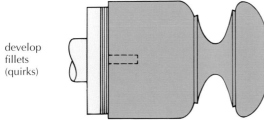

develop
fillets
(quirks)

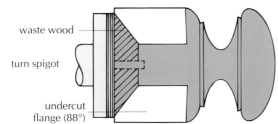

waste wood

turn spigot

undercut
flange (88°)

(Above) *Fig. 84 A typical Victorian knob for a chest of drawers.*

Fig. 85 Turning stages for a simple knob.

Method

1. If more than one identical knob is to be turned, make a turning guide and a template. This will make turning quicker and easier and ensure that the finished knobs are of the same size and shape.

2. Prepare a blank of wood 1⅜ × 1⅜ × 3in (60 × 60 × 76mm) in your chosen wood; mark the centre at one end and centre pop.

3. Drill a suitable pilot hole, using a bench drill, of the appropriate diameter and depth for your particular screw chuck. Screw the blank on to the screw chuck with a ply spacer placed between the work and the face of the chuck.

4. Screw the chuck on to the headstock of the lathe; set the lathe speed to 2,000rpm. Move the tailstock back out of the way as it will not be needed, and position the toolrest. Check that the work revolves freely before commencing to turn.

5. With the roughing-out gouge turn the blank to the round to 2⅛in (54mm)

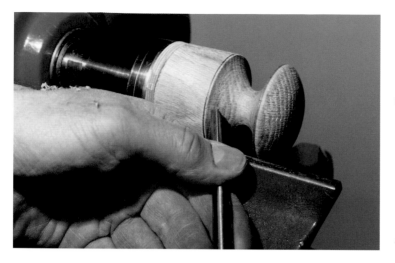

diameter. Adjust the toolrest parallel to the face of the work and true off the face with a spindle gouge.

6. Mark two lines clearly in pencil, one at ½in (13mm) from the outer face and one at 1½in (38mm), as shown in the drawing, and shape the domed top of the knob with the spindle gouge.

7. Using a ⅜in (10mm) spindle gouge start developing the cove half-way between the two lines, and form a waist ¾in (18mm) in diameter.

8. Form the two fillets each side of the waist using a ⅛in (3mm) parting tool, and then tidy up the curves that flow into the fillets using the spindle gouge.

9. Turn the spigot to the required diameter with

(Top) *Fig. 86 Turning the waist with a ⅜in (10mm) spindle gouge. Always cut down the slope and keep the bevel close to the wood.*

(Above) *Fig. 87 Turning the fillet with a ⅛in (3mm) parting tool.*

Fig. 88 Turning the spigot with the ⅛in (3mm) parting tool.

Fig. 89 Checking the diameter of the spigot with Vernier callipers. Always switch off the lathe for this operation, otherwise the callipers could be caught in the wood and swing round towards the turner, causing injury.

a parting tool and a spindle gouge, making sure that the underside of the flange is undercut. Do not part off the knob on the lathe; the waste wood can be cut off by hand at a later stage. In this way it is a simple job to rechuck the work should any tidying up become necessary.

10. Sand using a range of grits from 240 through to 400, and finish with fine, non-woven web abrasive. Take care not

to round off the fillets, which should be crisp. The knob can be stained and polished, on or off the lathe, as desired.

REPAIRING A KNOB WITH A PARTIALLY DAMAGED FLANGE

Often it is just the flange of the knob that is damaged. On the principle that it is always best to replace only the minimum amount of wood, the turner can opt to graft on a

Fig. 90 A drawer knob with a partially damaged flange.

new piece of wood. This may be time-consuming but it is well worth saving a nicely made knob, with its original patina, wherever possible.

Each type of knob presents the turner with a different challenge. If the knob has a wooden spigot then there is a good chance that the spigot can be held in a three- or four-jaw chuck. Some adjustment with thin slivers of wood or card may be necessary to ensure that the work runs absolutely true. Knobs that have an iron bolt rather than a spigot, however, pose a different problem. There is a very good chance that the bolt will have corroded into the wood, and it is virtually impossible to remove it without splitting the knob. Many bolts have square shoulders designed to go through a square hole in the drawer front, so that the knob could not twist round and work loose. It would be almost impossible to hold such a knob in a three- or four-jaw chuck and get it to run true. However, the method described below, which uses a glue chuck, does work well.

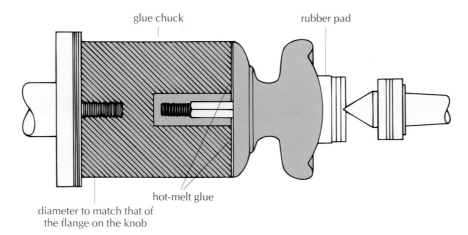

glue chuck   rubber pad

hot-melt glue

diameter to match that of the flange on the knob

(Above) *Fig. 91 Repairing a partially damaged knob flange.*

Fig. 92 Planing off the jagged edge to produce a clean, flat surface.

80

Method

1. First plane off the jagged edge on the broken flange to produce a clean, smooth surface. Glue on a suitable small piece of wood to form the graft. If PVA adhesive is used you should cramp up and leave plenty of time for the glue to cure, or use a super glue or epoxy resin glue, which will cure quickly. When the bond has formed, trim away the excess wood to reduce the risk of the tool catching when the graft is turned.

2. Take a piece of scrap wood to form a glue chuck and turn a cylinder 2¼in (57mm) long with a diameter to match the flange on the knob. Face off the blank. Place a drill chuck, with the appropriate MT shank, in the tailstock and select a drill bit which is ¼in (6mm) larger in diameter than the iron bolt. The larger hole will give greater clearance and allow for the fact that the bolt may not be exactly in the centre of the knob. Drill the hole to a depth just longer than the bolt.

3. Take the knob and marry it up to the glue chuck, making sure that the flange seats snugly; it may be necessary to slope the front of the glue chuck slightly to match the underside of the flange.

4. Place three small blobs of hot-melt glue equally spaced around the drilled hole of the glue chuck, taking care not to get glue actually in the hole, and position the knob so that it is held firmly. The hot-melt glue should give sufficient adhesion to last through the turning.

5. Rotate the headstock spindle by hand to make sure that the knob is running true. If it is not, take it off and try again! Set the lathe speed to 2,000rpm. Bring up the tailstock to give support and fit a revolving centre with some form of rubber pad so that it will not mark the domed surface of the knob.

6. Position the toolrest and turn the new wood very carefully to shape using a sharp ¼in (6mm) spindle gouge until the grafted area matches the rest of the flange. Sand gently.

Fig. 93 Turning the spliced-on wood to match the profile of the flange with a spindle gouge. For the purpose of this photograph a light wood has been used to show the graft clearly. In reality a matching dark wood was used. The glue chuck has been coloured green to show the knob more clearly. Note the use of the multi-head revolving centre in the tailstock with a cup chuck, padded with foam, to support the end of the knob.

Fig. 94 Using a thin parting tool firstly to turn the back of the graft, and then to part off the completed knob from the glue chuck.

7. Now comes the tricky part – removing the knob from the glue chuck without damage! Use a thin parting tool to turn the back of the graft to match the host knob; then cut away the edge of the glue chuck until very little wood remains, and then gently twist the knob. It should come away cleanly with any residue of hot-melt glue left on the glue chuck. Some patience and skill will now be needed to stain and polish the new wood to match the old.

REPAIRING A KNOB WHEN THE WHOLE FLANGE IS DAMAGED

Sometimes the whole flange will have broken away, leaving a jagged ring of wood. The small, walnut knob in Fig. 95 was once on a desk drawer and was one of a pair. The knob had a spigot that was threaded three-quarters of the way, leaving a parallel area that allowed me to secure the spigot in a three-jaw drill chuck. The drill chuck had

Fig. 95 An example of a knob where the flange has completely broken off.

Fig. 96 Removing the remains of the old broken flange with a parting tool. The knob is held in a three-jaw drill chuck screwed on to the headstock spindle.

Fig. 97 Turning the new flange. Again a light wood has been used for the purposes of clarity. Take gentle cuts to avoid tearing the wood out of the chuck.

Method

1. With the knob mounted in the drill chuck remove the remains of the old flange with a spindle gouge. Remove the knob from the chuck.
2. Take a suitable piece of wood, the thickness of the flange, and drill a hole in the centre to match the diameter of the newly tidied-up stem. If you do not have exactly the right-sized drill, it is a simple job to enlarge the hole using a round file until a good, snug fit is achieved.
3. Cut the blank roughly to shape to reduce the risk of the turning tool catching. A powered fretsaw is very useful for this task as an accurate circle can be cut. The wood will now resemble a thick washer.

a capacity of ¾in (19mm) and was screwed directly on to the headstock, thus ensuring that it remained secure during turning.

4. Push the wood over the spigot on the knob and glue in position with PVA over the area where the flange is to be formed.

5. Remount the knob in the drill chuck. It is important that the knob should realign perfectly. It is a good idea to have a register mark permanently on the drill chuck, and this can be neatly done by drilling a shallow hole on the body of the chuck and filling it with paint. Just draw a pencil mark against the register mark on the wood to be rechucked before it is removed from the lathe: it is then a simple matter to match the marks up again.

6. Turn the new flange to shape, taking gentle cuts with a sharp ¼in (6mm) spindle gouge. Sand, stain and polish the new flange to match the rest of the knob.

FIXING METHODS

Very old knobs were often made with threaded spigots, which married with an appropriate thread in the drawer front. Sometimes it is the other way round and you find that the body of the knob is threaded and a threaded wooden screw is passed through the back of the drawer and into the knob to hold it in position. Alternatively, the knob has a parallel spigot, which passes through the front of the drawer and is glued in position; then a wedge is inserted into a cross cut in the spigot to give a good, tight fit. Many old knobs have an iron nut and bolt, which can be solid with rust, posing a problem if the knob is loose or damaged and needs to be removed. Often the hole to take the spigot or fixing has become enlarged and damaged. In a great deal of contemporary furniture the knob is simply screwed in position from behind with a wood screw. A parallel spigot inserted and merely glued into a hole is not a very reliable method and in time the knob will loosen and come away.

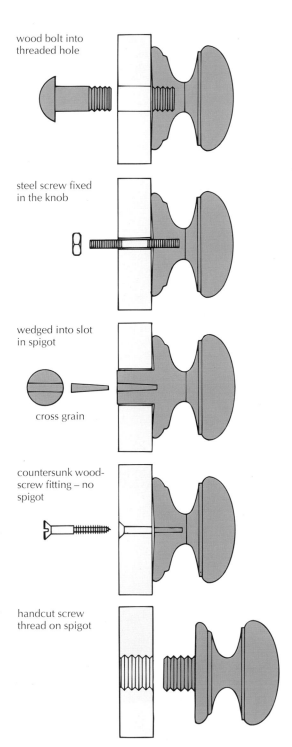

wood bolt into threaded hole

steel screw fixed in the knob

wedged into slot in spigot

cross grain

countersunk wood-screw fitting – no spigot

handcut screw thread on spigot

Fig. 98 Five methods for fixing knobs to a host unit.

9

Legs and Feet

CHAIR AND STOOL LEGS

Turning a leg or a stretcher for a chair or stool is a typical repair task. Chair legs and stretchers often become damaged and you will surely be asked by friends and family alike to turn up the odd replacement 'when you have a spare moment'! As I keep stressing, it is essential to plan the work before commencing to turn, otherwise it will be virtually impossible to turn more than one item of the same shape. The illustration below shows a detailed plan of a Windsor chair leg with datum lines and diameters clearly marked. When turning more than one spindle it is a good idea to make a full-sized template, and I refer the reader back to Chapter 7.

In the first example I have chosen a chair leg based on an American Windsor chair of early nineteenth-century design. The basic rules are that curves should be full and well rounded-out and not scant or flat, and that the connection between a

Fig. 99 A collection of damaged chair legs and stretchers.

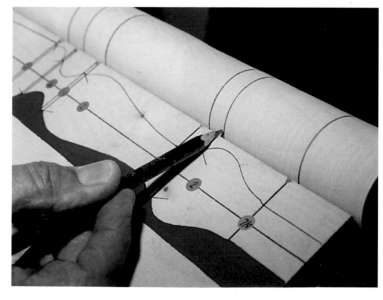

Fig. 100 Using a template to position the datum lines on the turned cylinder.

curve and a fillet should be as close to a right angle as possible to produce a crisp change of direction.

A WINDSOR CHAIR LEG

1. Cut a blank from well-seasoned wood 18 ⅛in (460mm) long × 2¼in (57mm) square, mark the centres on each end and centre punch. The example shown in the photographs was turned in sycamore.
2. Fit a revolving centre in the tailstock and a ring centre in the headstock and set the lathe speed at 2,000rpm. Mount the spindle blank between centres and tighten the tailstock. Position the tool-rest just below centre height and secure. Check by hand that the spindle rotates freely without catching on the toolrest.
3. Using the roughing-out gouge, turn the spindle to the round to just over

2in (50mm) in diameter. Take the template and lay the edge against the turned cylinder, then mark the datum lines with a pencil as the lathe rotates.
4. Using the roughing-out gouge, turn the 8½in (216mm) long taper in gentle stages, keeping the bevel close to the wood for the final cut. Use Vernier callipers to check the relevant diameters.
5. Next take the spindle gouge and form the centre cove. It is essential that the gouge is sharp, and it will need to be kept sharp during the turning. Always cut downhill! Develop the fillets and then form the bead.
6. Go back if necessary and finish off the centre cove. It is always better to take off too little rather than too much. Develop the shapes until the final form and diameters are achieved, even if this means going back to a previous stage.
7. Turn the two baluster shapes, keeping the bevel close to the wood.

TOP HALF

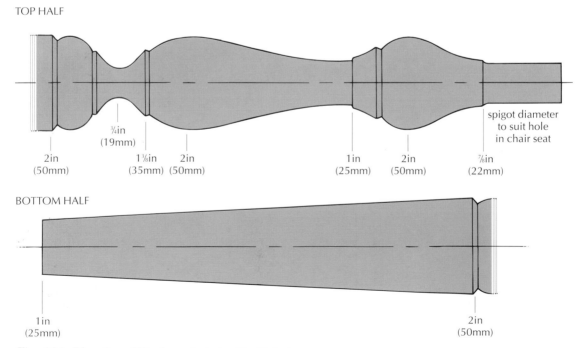

BOTTOM HALF

Fig. 101 Plan for a Windsor chair leg (half size).

Fig. 102 Forming the bead.

Fig. 103 Turning the baluster shape with a ⅜in (10mm) spindle gouge.

8. Leave the spigot at the top of the leg slightly larger in diameter than required. The leg can be remounted just before fitting into the seat and the desired amount spun off to ensure a good fit in the hole.

9. When you are satisfied with the shape and diameters and have used the template as a double check, remove the toolrest and commence sanding, working from 280 grit through to 400 grit and finishing off with non woven web abrasive. Keep the abrasive moving to avoid the build-up of lines, and give a final burnish with a handful of shavings. Wear a disposable mask when sanding.

10. Make any other legs to match and if necessary remount a leg that may need further attention. Be critical. If you are not critical someone else is sure to be!

Fig. 104 The finished leg ready for staining.

CHAIR STRETCHERS

Stretchers take a great deal of punishment and are often broken. Some have a very simple tapered shape and others are more ornate, but in each case the design is symmetrical from the centre to each end. In the example shown in the photograph below the stretchers came from several matching country chairs and I used the broken stretcher as my guide. Care was taken to ensure that the ends were turned to match the appropriate holes in the chair legs. Again the ring centre was used to drive the wood, so that the stretchers could

Fig. 105 A typical broken chair stretcher.

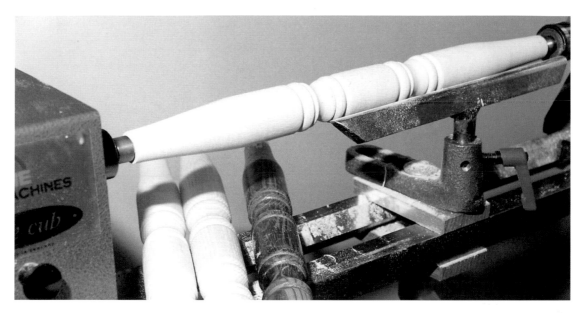

Fig. 106 The final stretcher on the lathe.

be remounted if necessary. Provided that the wood is cut to the correct length and care is taken to check diameters, it is a relatively easy turning operation and is well within the scope of the average lathe. A new stretcher can give a chair many more years of useful life.

STOOLS

When I was writing this book, and looking for suitable examples to illustrate the various techniques, I found a small oak stool with two stick legs and two turned legs in a junk shop, and I took it back to the workshop with the intention of turning up two

Fig. 107 The stool with its odd assortment of legs.

Fig. 108 Even the two turned legs were different!

Fig. 109 Plan for legs and top for a small stool.

legs to replace the stick legs. On closer examination, I found even the two turned legs were different! Three of the legs came out of their holes with a simple twist of the wrist but one leg was very difficult to remove, as it had an iron nail well embedded. It soon became obvious that the top of the stool was riddled with woodworm that was beyond treatment. I rather liked the stool, however, and decided to copy it.

You may need to replace one leg or several on a stool, or, alternatively, the legs may be satisfactory but a new top may be required. The following instructions cover both possibilities but obviously the dimensions given are only meant as a guide because each stool will differ.

Legs
1. First make a simple turning guide in card or thin ply; this is particularly

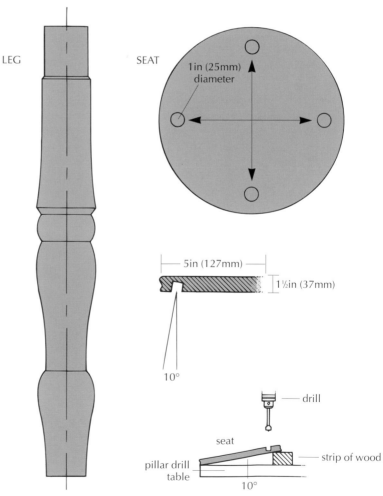

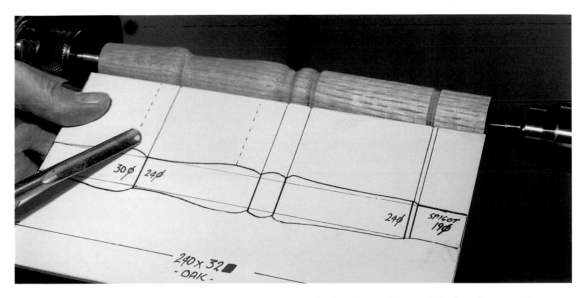

Fig. 110 A carefully produced turning guide was made for the stool legs, with the relevant diameters and the position of each cut marked on.

important if more than one leg is to be turned. If you have a damaged leg to cut in half to produce a template so much the better.

2. Prepare four blanks 1¼ × 1¼ × 9½in (32 × 32 × 241mm). Mark the centres, and centre pop, at each end.

3. Fit a ring centre in the headstock and a revolving centre in the tailstock, and mount a blank between centres. I recommend using a ring centre when turning spindles because the ring leaves a clear indentation on the wood and this makes it very easy to remount a spindle accurately should this be necessary at a later stage. Position the toolrest and check that the blank revolves without obstruction.

4. First rough out the blank to produce a cylinder, and then shape with a spindle gouge. Turn the spigot slightly larger in diameter than the hole it is intended to fit. Use the turning guide and a pair of callipers as an aid throughout the turning process to make sure that both the dimensions and the shape are correct.

5. Repeat the sequence to produce four matching legs.

Top

1. Prepare a blank for the top of the stool from a piece of 1½in (38mm) thick wood 10 × 10in (254 × 254mm). Mark a centre point and draw a circle with a pair of compasses.

2. Produce a roughly round shape by cutting the corners off the blank using a bandsaw or a hand saw.

3. Drill a suitable pilot hole for a screw chuck and mount the blank with a spacer between the wood and the face of the chuck. A screw chuck will only leave one central hole to fill rather than the four left when a faceplate is used. A lathe with a swivelling headstock will probably be needed to turn a blank of this diameter unless the lathe has sufficient swing over the bed bars.

4. Screw the chuck to the headstock, position the toolrest and set the lathe speed to 800rpm. Face off the front of the

blank with a spindle gouge and finish with a round-nosed scraper to achieve a smooth, level surface.

5. Reposition the toolrest and turn the outside edge. Turn a slightly concave groove using a ⅜in (10mm) spindle gouge.

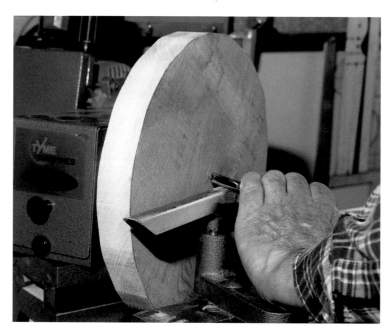

Fig. 111 Facing off the front of the blank for a new stool top.

Remove the toolrest and sand both the surface and the edge. Start with 180 grit and work through to 400 grit.

6. Replace the toolrest and position it parallel with the face and cut three decorative V rings with a gouge or the long point of a skew. Remove the toolrest and deburr the edges of the Vs. Rub the whole surface with non-woven abrasive and burnish with a handful of shavings.

Drilling the Holes in the Top for the Legs

1. Mark the positions of the four holes accurately on the underside of the stool top and centre punch each spot.
2. Cramp a strip of wood across the table of the drill press so that, when the top is rested on the wood, holes can be drilled at an angle of 10

Fig. 112 Drilling the holes for the legs at an angle. Note the piece of wood cramped across the table, and the angle-setter.

degrees (or whatever angle is required). A bubble spirit angle is useful to set up the correct angle.

3. Mark the curve of the stool top on the strip of wood with a felt pen so that it can be positioned accurately ready to drill each hole. This is a satisfactory method for a one-off stool but it is worth making a hinged sloping table to speed up the process if you are making lots of stools and chairs.

4. Fit a ¾in (19mm) saw-tooth Forstner bit in the drill press and set the depth stop so that the drill will not break through the top surface. It is worth making a trial hole in a scrap piece of wood of a similar thickness to make sure that the depth is correct. If an old leg is going into a new top then a hole to match the size of the spigot will obviously have to be drilled.

Assembly

1. Remount each leg in turn and spin off the spigot until a good fit is achieved for that particular hole. Wood not only moves but drilled holes often vary slightly in diameter, and the aim here is to get a tight fit.

2. Glue in each leg. If you are merely replacing a leg, make sure that the existing hole is cleaned out and free from any old glue. The same applies if old legs are going into a new top. The top of the spigot on the leg needs to be clean. Do not attempt to remount an old leg to spin down the spigot because it is very unlikely to run true. It is better to hand sand or pare away small slivers of wood until the spigot fits the hole tightly. Stain or finish the wood as required.

TABLE LEGS

I will explain three possible ways to repair or replace a broken or damaged table leg. Option one is to turn a completely new leg,

option two is to splice on a piece of new wood, and option three is to replace only a section of the leg; the last two options may be particularly desirable if the table is antique and of value.

A NEW PINE KITCHEN TABLE LEG

Domestic tables are often obtainable at low cost from sales and junk shops but they may well need one, or several, new legs. The instructions below describe how to make a typical pine kitchen table leg, and some suggested dimensions are given with a plan in Fig. 113. Obviously if you are only replacing one leg the design must match the remaining legs, but the method and techniques will be the same.

Stage 1

1. First make a simple turning guide to show where the initial and subsequent V cuts are positioned, and write on the relevant diameters at various points along the leg.

2. Prepare a blank $28 \times 3 \times 3$in ($711 \times 76 \times 76$mm) in PAR pine. It is very important that the wood is planed absolutely square: do not attempt to do this afterwards! Draw diagonals at both ends of the blank to find the centre, and centre pop.

3. Fit a ring centre in the headstock and a revolving centre in the tailstock, and set the lathe speed to 1,200rpm. Use your longest toolrest.

4. With the blank mounted in the lathe, mark off 6in (150mm) at the headstock end and place wide masking tape along the line. The tape has two uses: it acts as a clear guide to mark where the first cut is to be made and it also protects the square edges against chipping and splintering during turning.

Stage 2

1. Set the toolrest so that the centre is in line with the position of the first V cut at A.

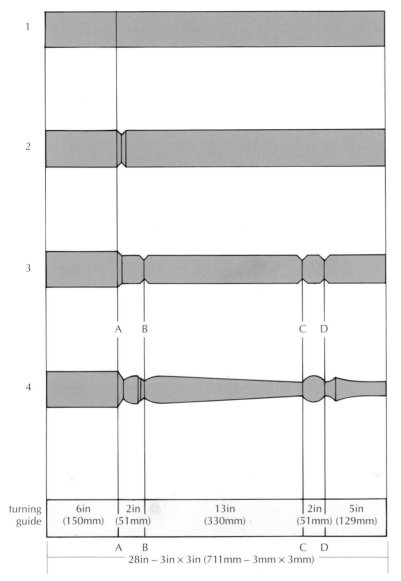

Fig. 113 Stages in making a kitchen table leg.

	6in (150mm)	2in (51mm)	13in (330mm)	2in (51mm)	5in (129mm)

turning guide

A B   C D

28in – 3in × 3in (711mm – 3mm × 3mm)

(Below) Fig. 114 Use tape to mark the extent of the square top and to protect the edges from damage.

2. Check that the work rotates freely, and with the long point of a skew cut the initial V to the depth required.

Stage 3

1. Reset the toolrest and start turning the rest of the leg to a round cylinder, using a roughing-out gouge. The toolrest will need to be moved along to complete the cut.
2. Increase the lathe speed to 2,000rpm for the rest of the turning.
3. Take the turning guide and mark on the turned cylinder the positions of the three remaining Vs at B, C and D. Cut the Vs with the long point of a skew.

Fig. 115 Cutting the initial V with the long point of a skew chisel. Note how the tape ensures the correct position for the cut.

Fig. 116 A turning guide used to mark the positions of the three remaining Vs.

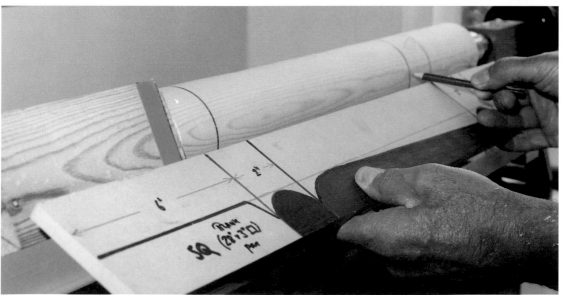

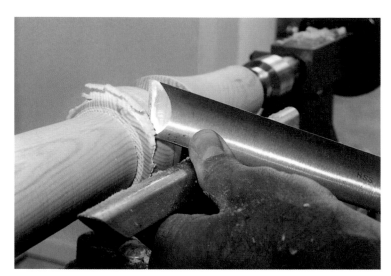

Fig. 117 Forming the bead with the oval skew chisel.

Fig. 118 Checking the diameter with callipers.

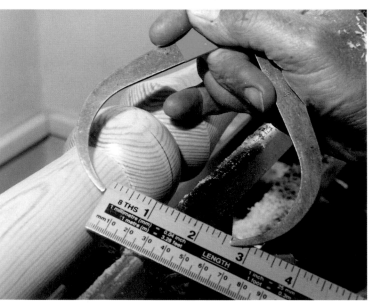

Stage 4

1. Using a roughing-out gouge develop the centre baluster shape between B and C, and finish the cut with a skew.
2. Shape the foot in a similar way between D and the end of the blank.
3. Form the bead between C and D with a skew or a ⅜in (10mm) spindle gouge, taking time to develop a well-shaped bead.
4. Turn the shape between A and B with the skew and form the fillet with a parting tool or skew.
5. Check the diameters and make any tidying cuts as required. Remove the toolrest, move the banjo out of the way and sand and burnish the finished leg.
6. When turning any subsequent matching legs, follow exactly the same sequence and develop the curves using the same chisels; check each diameter carefully and make a visual comparison to ensure that the legs are as near identical as possible.

SPLICING ON NEW WOOD

Sometimes it is only necessary to replace part of a leg, which may have been damaged by rot, worm or by animals chewing at the wood. Grafting on a piece of new wood should not drastically affect the value of a piece of furniture because it is accepted that the bottoms of legs will become damaged over the years, where replacing the whole leg could well reduce the value. The technique described here is a very useful one, which can be applied to other partially damaged spindles.

For an example I chose a slender mahogany leg from a card table, the bottom 5in (13cm) of which had been chewed by a puppy! Only the front half needed replacing as the back of the leg was free from any teeth marks. It was a simple matter to cut out the damaged portion, making sure that the horizontal cut lined up with the bead so that the join could be disguised. This is not always possible, and sometimes a

diagonal cut is less obvious. The piece of wood chosen for the graft needed to be of a similar quality and grain pattern as the original and fortunately I had a piece of suitable old mahogany. The new wood was glued in position and the leg cramped up.

The most difficult part of this operation proved to be mounting the leg between centres so that it ran true. Merely centre popping the ends was not accurate enough, so great care needed to be taken. I used a ring centre in the headstock to hold the foot of the leg in order to reduce the risk of the wood splitting, and I fitted a

Fig. 119 The chewed bottom of an eighteenth-century mahogany leg.

Fig. 120 The damaged area has been cut away and a piece of mahogany glued in place, ready for turning.

Fig. 121 The repaired leg ready for staining.

Fig. 122 The leg with the crushed portion cut off.

revolving centre in the tailstock. When the lathe was switched on the silhouette of the original shape became visible and I turned the grafted wood so that it exactly matched the shape of the original using a roughing out gouge, a ⅜in (10mm) spindle gouge and a ½in (13mm) oval skew. I took my time, stopping the lathe often to see what was happening. A piece of white card placed behind the turning can be very helpful, and it is certainly necessary to have good light. I started with the lathe running at 1,200rpm and finished at 2,000rpm.

Rather than sand the finished graft in the lathe, which would have removed some of the stained and polished surface of the remaining half of the leg, I hand sanded the new wood. This hand sanding also ensured that the graft did not look too crisp and new. I delivered the repaired leg to the restorer, who worked his magic so that it was soon difficult to see the graft at all. Obviously this technique will only be suitable if the leg can be removed from the table! If this is not the case then the third option (described below) may be the only possibility.

REPLACING A SECTION OF THE LEG

Occasionally a slender leg will snap completely, or, as stated above, it may not be possible to remove a partially damaged leg from a table. In the example shown, the top 4in (10cm) of a leg needed replacing because it was crushed beyond repair.

The first thing I did was to cut the leg cleanly across and remove the damaged section. Always aim to make the cut at the start of a bead or fillet if possible so that the join will be disguised. It is possible to make a diagonal cut but this is more difficult; a possible method is described in Chapter 12. I deliberately used a lighter wood for the replacement section so that it would show up clearly in the photograph, but the final repair was

carried out with a piece of old mahogany. I turned up the new piece of leg and checked that the diameter matched accurately.

To reinforce the join, a dowel (metal or wooden are both possible) was placed inside a drilled hole down the centre of the leg. It is always difficult to drill an accurate hole in the middle of a round section of a spindle because drills have a habit of wandering and following the grain of the wood. The method I normally use is to drill a hole in the two pieces to be joined with a larger diameter than that of the dowel to be inserted. For this particular leg I drilled a hole ⅜in (10mm) in diameter to a depth of 2½in (64mm) to take a 5in (127mm) steel dowel, with a diameter of ¼in (6mm). A metal dowel is stronger than an equivalent wooden dowel and threaded steel rod is available in a wide variety of diameters from DIY outlets and can be used effectively. I carried out the drilling operation in a floor-standing pillar drill but it could equally be done with a hand or powered drill; indeed,

Fig. 123 Drilling the replacement portion of the leg to take the other end of the steel dowel.

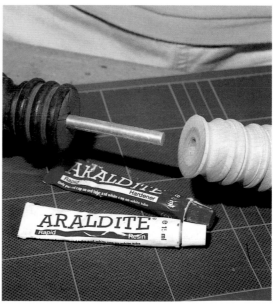

Fig. 124 Gluing the metal dowel in place with epoxy resin.

this would have to be the case if the leg could not be removed from the table.

Because the holes were larger than the dowel it was not difficult to align the two parts. Firstly the holes were filled with epoxy resin and then the two parts, with the rod in position, were pushed together and lined up accurately. Masking tape can be used to hold the joint whilst the adhesive cures. Any excess epoxy should be wiped off before it has the chance to set. Although the epoxy gave latitude it must be stressed that the holes still need to be drilled as accurately as possible in the centre of each half and along their particular axis. This method makes a good strong repair.

FEET

Turned feet, found on armchairs, sofas, beds, chests of drawers and other items of furniture, are subject to damage over the years, and replacements may be needed. Because feet on furniture spend most of their long life in contact with the floor, woodworm infestation and damp are often causes of damage.

On a woodwormed surface only a few flight holes may indicate the real problem inside. The first hint of trouble is usually when a little dust appears on the floor, but this can be easily missed. Clearly the sooner a worm problem is detected and treated the better, before the infestation spreads to the carcass. Where damp is the problem the wood eventually rots away and the foot collapses.

The sideways, dragging movement of heavy, loaded furniture will also place considerable strain on feet. Screws from castor plates may crack the timber, which becomes brittle as central heating dries out the wood, and subsequent attempts to rectify the problem with screws and nails often exacerbate the damage.

For any of these reasons you may wish to replace a turned, damaged foot, or indeed a set of feet. If one or more feet have survived then the job is straightforward. Armed with a profile gauge, callipers, ruler, paper and pencil it should not be difficult to produce a template or a plan for turning the replacement. Moreover, this planning work can be done *in situ* without the item having to be moved to the workshop.

Fig. 125 *A selection of antique feet.*

If all the feet are missing, there is nothing to guide the turner as to form or dimension. It should also be remembered that existing feet may not be original and a close look at the underside of the item of furniture should reveal some clues. For example, a chest of drawers or a long-case clock may have had their bracket feet replaced with bun feet at some stage as fashion changed, in which case signs of the previous fitting should be evident from holes, lighter wood or glue marks. In other words, it may not simply be a matter of copy turning; some idea of shape, form and dimension will be needed.

Feet, being at the bottom of a piece of furniture, are often obscured by shadow, thick carpet or loose covers and do not attract much attention. Detail is often lost in photographs and drawings in books on antique furniture. Moreover, only a writer or illustrator who is also a practical turner will include the necessary fine detail in sketches of turned items. However, the feet on a piece of furniture are an important part of the item as a whole and are not there just for decoration. Too small a foot on a large item will look wrong and so will a large foot on a small item. For purely practical reasons it is also most important that the foot should be strong enough to bear the weight of the carcass.

A WILLIAM AND MARY-STYLE FOOT

I chose to turn this particular foot as an example because it has an attractive shape. The foot measures 4in (102mm), excluding the spigot, and is 3in (76mm) at its maximum diameter; it is turned in fine-grain Brazilian mahogany. The spigot measures 1in (25mm) in diameter and is ¾in (19mm) long. This type of foot could well be found on a small table, a dressing table or a cabinet.

The first thing to do is to make a detailed template with the datum lines clearly marked. Then prepare a blank 3 × 3 × 4¾in (76 × 76 × 121mm). Mark the centres accurately and centre pop. Fit a four-prong drive centre in the headstock and a revolving centre in the tailstock, and set the lathe speed to 2,000rpm. With the wood mounted between centres, position the toolrest and check that the blank rotates without obstruction before turning the blank to the round with a roughing-out gouge. Refer to the turning stages shown in Fig. 127.

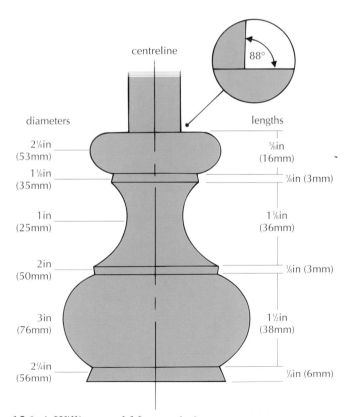

Fig. 126 A William and Mary-style foot.

Stage 1

With a parting tool, form a spigot at the tailstock end to the length and diameter required to suit the host item. Slightly undercut the flange at the top of the spigot so that the foot will seat properly when fitted into its hole.

Stage 2

With the lathe running, hold the template against the wood and mark the positions of the fillets with a pencil at A, B and C, and with the parting tool cut grooves into the cylinder to just above the final maximum diameter of the fillets.

Stage 3

Form the cove and the central waist with a ⅜in (10mm) spindle gouge. The minimum diameter of the waist is 1in (25mm). To give room to manoeuvre the gouge, reduce the diameter of the area above the waist.

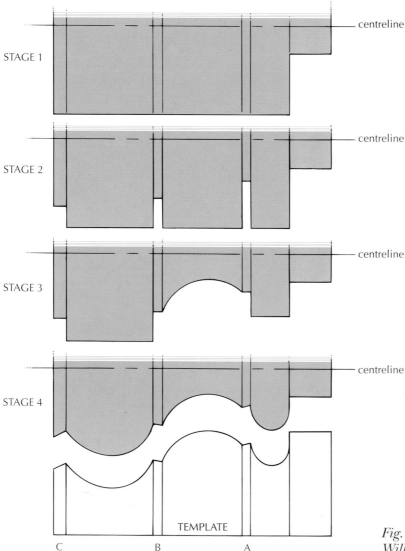

Fig. 127 Stages of turning a William and Mary-style foot.

Fig. 128 Forming the bun shape of a William and Mary-style foot with a skew.

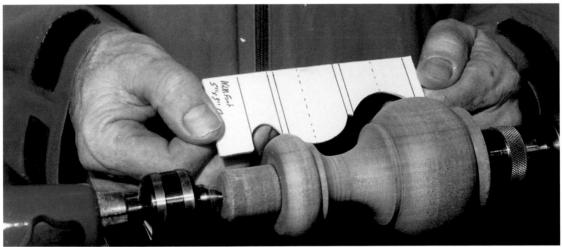

(Above) *Fig. 129 Checking the shape of the foot against the template.*

Fig. 130 The completed William and Mary-style foot ready for staining.

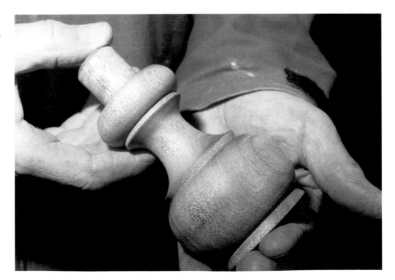

Stage 4
Form the bead at the top of the foot with the skew chisel, making sure that gentle cuts are taken to develop a symmetrical curve. Next form the bun shape using the skew, and finally complete the fillets at A, B and C, also with the skew. At each stage check with the template and measure with callipers. Finally remove the toolrest, sand and burnish the work, and stain and polish as required.

Fig. 131 The rather crude underside of a Davenport with one original foot still in position.

TURNING FEET FOR A DAVENPORT

A smaller bun foot is to be found on a Davenport – a desk with a sloping lid and drawers down one side. I was interested to read that the name of this piece of furniture is assumed to have arisen from Gillows Cost Books in the late eighteenth century, where the entry 'Captain Davenport, a desk' occurs, which is rather charming.

On the desk I was repairing, two of the feet still existed, and it was possible to use a profile gauge and callipers to produce a detailed drawing and template. The feet did not have a spigot, but screwed directly on to the carcass, so the replacements were turned on a screw chuck with a screw size to match the screw still in place on the Davenport. During fitting, a little sanding was needed on the flat surface of each foot to balance the Davenport, as the frame was somewhat warped; you will find this is quite often the case.

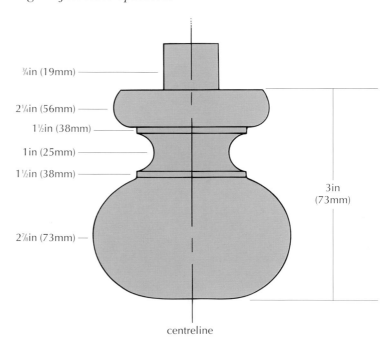

¾in (19mm)

2¼in (56mm)

1½in (38mm)

1in (25mm)

1½in (38mm)

2⅞in (73mm)

3in (73mm)

centreline

Fig. 132 Small bun foot for a Davenport.

Fig. 133 Using a template to check the shape of a replacement foot for a Davenport.

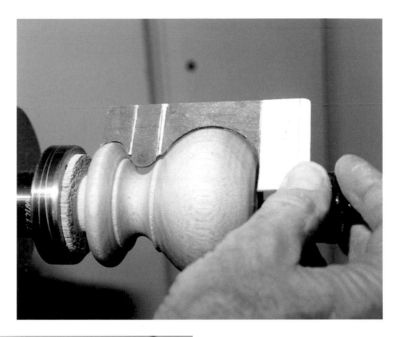

Fig. 134 Using a home-made diameter gauge to check the measurement of the waist.

furniture rely on a spike or a nail, while other pieces may have one or more wood screws either screwed up through the foot or screwed in from the top. A spigot fitting is by far the most satisfactory because with this method wood is bonded with wood to give a long-lasting joint, whereas metal, particularly steel and iron screws and nails, may rust and deteriorate over the years.

Often the problem is not the turning but the fixing! Clearly, if the host base is damaged this will need attention before the foot is attached. There is little point in turning up a new foot then trying to fix it to a worm-eaten or damaged carcass. Beds, sofas and heavy armchairs often have a turned bun foot fitted with a castor, which can make things more complicated. Only too often the bottom of the frame is

FITTING

Before drawing up a plan and template, decide how the foot is to be fitted to the carcass. Is it to have a spigot or not? Although most feet are joined to the host item by a spigot, some small items of old

Fig. 135 The completed feet on the repolished Davenport.

damaged as a result of previous repair attempts and it is difficult to find enough sound wood.

Sometimes the hole to take the spigot is damaged or enlarged. It is not enough just to fill the hole with a proprietary wood filler and hope for the best! You can either increase the size of the hole carefully with a carving gouge and turn the foot with a larger diameter spigot to match or you can turn a wooden plug to fill the hole, glue it in position and then redrill. The frame may be so poor that it is necessary to carry out some radical woodwork before fitting can take place

Adhesives for Fitting Feet

Animal glue is to be preferred for antique furniture as this is gap-filling and can be removed if further work is needed at some time in the future. Previous holes and surfaces should be cleaned out thoroughly in preparation for gluing. For more general work, when the spigot and hole are a good fit, PVA adhesive will be quite suitable.

10

Bases and Stands

Trophies, models, small figurines and similar items are usually mounted on a turned wooden base or a pedestal for display. A stand needs to raise the article above table height, but it should not be too big or too elaborate or it will detract attention from the item on display. Most bases were once made from ebony or black wood or ebonized hardwood. A stand will vary in size and form; sometimes it is necessary to leave room for silver shields to be added to record events and winners and this should be borne in mind at the design stage.

In this chapter I describe how I made a new stand for a model of a Fairey Napier Monoplane, which crashed in 1929 shortly after leaving Royal Air Force Cranwell attempting a record-breaking flight to South Africa. The model, made in brass and originally silver-plated, is used as a table decoration, and although most of the silver plating has worn off I resisted the temptation to polish the brass with cleaner. Most trophies have a round base, which can either be seated in a groove cut in the pedestal or they on a spigot. This aircraft model has a rim machined from a casting, and although the inside is irregular the outside is virtually round, so it will sit into a prepared groove. The aim is to ensure that the item to be displayed sits snugly and firmly on its base but that it can be removed for cleaning. Some trophies may have a central screw that can be used to secure the trophy to the base.

Fig. 136 The aircraft on its new base.

A BASE FOR A TROPHY

I decided to use an old piece of well-seasoned English oak for the base, which I felt would give warmth and character to the piece. I chose to use a combination chuck to hold the wood so that there were no holes in the bottom; however, holes can always be filled and covered with baize so this is not really a problem. First I mounted the blank between centres and turned it to the round, and then faced off the ends. I cut a dovetail spigot to suit the chuck, and then held the spigot in the standard chuck jaws for the rest of the turning. A groove was carefully cut to take the foot of the trophy. The lathe was stopped frequently and the groove and the foot married together until both fitted snugly, before the rest of the base was turned using a spindle gouge.

Fig. 137 Fitting the blank into the dovetail jaws of a combination chuck.

Fig. 138 Cutting a groove to take the foot of the trophy.

Fig. 139 Checking that the foot fits accurately into the recess.

Fig. 140 An ornament displayed in a glass dome.

A BASE FOR A GLASS DOME

Small, delicate china figurines, models and stuffed birds are often protected under a glass dome, which can be round or oval in section. Occasionally one comes across a dome that has survived while the base is lost or riddled with woodworm. To turn up a replacement round base is quite straight-forward – an oval one is another story! Sometimes the item to be displayed is screwed into the base, or it may sit unsecured on a baize surface. In the example illustrated, a plinth was made to take a 5in (13cm) round dome. From the design point of view the base should be solid and nicely proportioned, and should enable the dome to sit securely in a small recess with a lip to ensure that it is not easily dislodged. Three small ball feet on the underside will make the whole display case easier to lift off a flat surface. Any hardwood will be suitable, and it can be stained if desired.

First I cut a blank with a diameter at least 1in (25mm) greater than the outside diameter of the dome I used and slightly thicker than the final thickness I required. The blank can be held on a faceplate or screw chuck, or in a combination chuck. I used a glue chuck to hold the blank temporarily whilst turning it to the round, and squared off the base prior to cutting a dovetail recess for a combination chuck.

With the blank mounted in the expansion mode I turned the face so that it was smooth and flat. The inside diameter of the glass dome was then marked on the surface and a cut made with the parting tool to form a lip matching the inside diameter of the dome to a depth of ½in (13mm). Using a ⅜in (10mm) spindle gouge, I shaped the outer edge of the plinth. I stained the sanded base using a Georgian Mahogany spirit stain and left it on the lathe overnight so that it could be friction polished the next day. Finally, I turned three small ball feet, stained them and screwed them to the underside of the stand, and cut a circle of red baize to sit on the top surface.

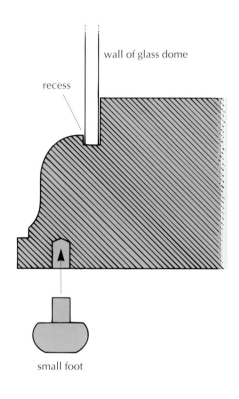

wall of glass dome

recess

small foot

Fig. 141 Base for a glass dome.

Fig. 142 Shaping the rest of the base.

Fig. 143 The sandglass with its broken spindles.

A STAND FOR A SANDGLASS

Sandglasses ('hourglass' is not the correct term), have a long history and played an important role in the measuring of the distance travelled and the speed of a ship, which in turn enabled the sailors to estimate their position at sea. Today they make an attractive ornament and there is something fascinating about watching the sand gradually trickle through from the top to the bottom. With the sandglass in my example, it was possible to lower the glass down through the top into a small indentation in the base and then to secure it in position with a disc with a matching indentation in the top.

As you can clearly see from the photograph, all three spindles of the sandglass were broken beyond repair but the top and base were intact, if somewhat distressed! This was a simple country turning in pine

with the minimum of decoration but still worth undertaking. The work involved turning three new replacement spindles and a centre piece for the top disc to hold the sandglass in position. It is important to ensure that the completed structure enables the glass to move slightly to allow for the movement of the wood but it must be strong enough to withstand handling and constant inverting. Some sandglasses have small feet at the top and bottom of each spindle but there were no signs of any in this particular design. The number of spindles can also vary.

Replacement glass domes and sandglasses in various sizes are available from specialist turning suppliers.

Fig. 144 The renovated sandglass.

A NEW BASE FOR A POLE SCREEN

Pole screens were popular from the eighteenth century onwards, and were used to protect ladies from the heat radiated by an open fire, which probably melted their make-up! The screens consisted of a base, or tripod legs, a short pillar and a narrow, tall pole, usually with a decorative finial on top. A screen, often embroidered, was attached to the pole by a bracket so that it could be moved up or down as required.

The mahogany pole screen I use as an example in this chapter is a late eighteenth-century one I was given to restore. The brief was to turn a base, 13in (330mm) in diameter, from a blank built up from laminated segments of mahogany. Three small bun feet were also required and a pillar 8in (203mm) long with a maximum diameter of 3in (76mm) to hold the pole. A very rough sketch was provided with copious notes in very small writing: the owner was an antique restorer who was very particular about detail and knew exactly what he wanted! In this chapter I will describe how I made the laminated base, the bun feet and the pillar, and how I cut a new bead to replace the damaged one on the pole. Fortunately my job was simply to turn the parts, not to stain and polish them!

THE BASE

1. The first layer of the base was made from one piece of ⅝in (16mm) thicknessed mahogany measuring 13in (330mm) in diameter. The next three

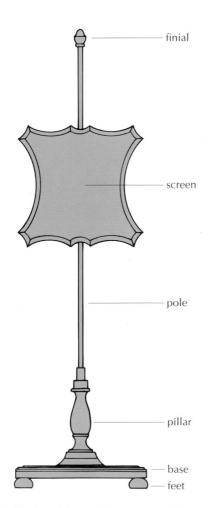

Fig. 145 An eighteenth-century pole screen.

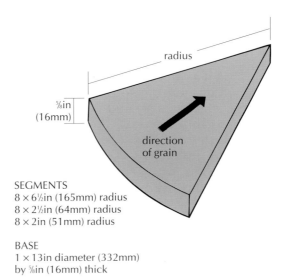

SEGMENTS
8 × 6½in (165mm) radius
8 × 2½in (64mm) radius
8 × 2in (51mm) radius

BASE
1 × 13in diameter (332mm)
by ⅝in (16mm) thick

Fig. 146 Segments cut to form the pole screen base.

Fig. 147 Using a card template to mark out segments with the wood grain running length-ways. The object is to waste as little mahogany as possible.

Fig. 148 Check that the segments fit together. Some trimming with a plane or a disc sander will be necessary. The segments are glued to the base, and to each other, with PVA glue and left cramped up overnight.

ensure that the grain of the wood always ran lengthwise and that there was a minimum wastage of timber. I cut the segments out on a powered fretsaw and then trued up the edges on a disc sander.

2. I laid the first layer of segments on the top of the single piece to check that they fitted accurately and planed up the edges as necessary. These segments were glued in place with PVA and cramped up. The same procedure was carried out with the remaining layers, allowing plenty of time for the glue to cure in each case. Each layer was arranged so that it overlapped the previous one to ensure maximum strength.

3. I then screwed the laminated blank to a screw chuck and mounted it on a lathe with the headstock swivelled round to allow sufficient clearance for a blank with a 13in (330mm) diameter. The lathe speed was set at 450rpm. Remember, the larger the blank, the slower the speed!

layers were built up from segments of ⅝in (16mm) thicknessed mahogany, rather like wedges of cheese, at an angle of 45 degrees. All together there were:

8 segments of 6½in (165mm) radius
8 of 2½in (64mm) radius
8 of 2in (51mm) radius

To aid marking out, card templates were cut, which could be laid on the thicknessed mahogany and arranged to

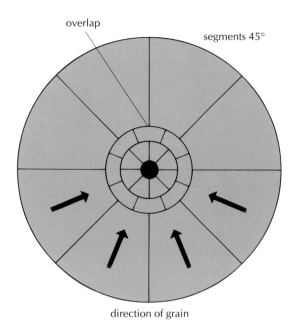

Fig. 149 Layers of segments for a pole screen base, viewed from above.

4. The blank was then turned, with a gouge, to the shape illustrated in Fig. 150. After sanding, I brushed off all the wood dust, and filled any small gaps between the segments with mahogany wood filler, which was left to harden overnight. The following day the work was sanded and burnished and a careful, final, check was made to see if any further filling was necessary.

5. Finally, using a beading tool, I cut a central hole with a diameter of 1in (25mm) and a depth of 1½in (38mm) to take the pillar spigot.

FEET

1. I turned three small bun feet 1in × 2in (25 × 51mm) from blanks of mahogany to the shape shown in Fig. 150.

2. The feet were fitted to the base by means of a central wood screw through a countersunk hole.

PILLAR

1. The central pillar was also turned from a blank of mahogany 8 × 3 × 3in (203 × 76 × 76mm). The centres were marked and punched. An expanding drill bit was set to match the diameter of the base of the existing pole and I made several trial cuts

Fig. 150 Base for a pole screen.

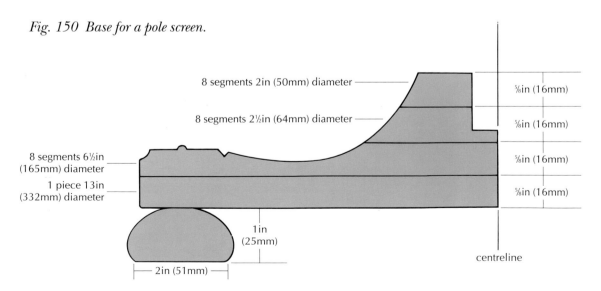

in scrap wood first to make sure that the setting selected was correct so that the pole fitted snugly. When I was quite happy with the size of hole I held the blank in a machine vice and, using a pillar drill, drilled a hole to a depth of 1½in (38mm).

2. I fitted a ring centre in the headstock and a large revolving centre in the tailstock so that the revolving centre cone supported the drilled hole.

3. The baluster-shaped pillar was then turned using a roughing-out gouge, a spindle gouge and a skew, and a parting tool was used to form a 1 × 1 ⅜in long (25 × 35mm) spigot at the base. The pillar was sanded and burnished before it was removed from the lathe, and was then glued into the base.

(Top) *Fig. 151 Turning the base with a bowl gouge. The blank is held on a faceplate.*

(Above) *Fig. 152 Shaping the pillar with a skew chisel.*

Fig. 153 The pillar spigot glued into the hole in the base.

THE BEAD

1. Because the turned bead at the bottom of the otherwise sound pole was damaged I decided to turn off the existing bead and turn a new one in its place. This presented the problem of how to hold a long spindle in the lathe without causing any further damage. I first made a jam chuck to hold the bottom of the pole securely in the headstock. Because the pole was considerably longer than the lathe, I made a simple, temporary steady to act as a cradle, and stapled rubber webbing over the pole to hold it in position. I applied plenty of wax to act as a lubricant to stop the wood burning as the friction built up.

2. I turned off the old bead with a small skew chisel and turned a new one just below it. The jam chuck ensured that the end of the pole was not damaged or crushed, and although the turning only took a few moments, it was well worth preparing the jam chuck and cradle.

Although this may be a rather unusual turning task, which you may not need to do yourself, a base such as this is strong, stable and attractive. It is economical with wood and makes a suitable base for a standard lamp, a plant stand or a small circular table.

Fig. 154 *Checking that the end of the pole fits snugly into the hole drilled in the top of the pillar.*

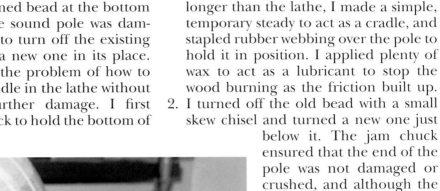

Fig. 155 *The end of the pole is held in a home-made jam chuck, so that the damaged bead can be turned off and a new one cut in its place.*

11

Decorative Turning

POST TOPS

Decorative tops often adorn and cover the end grain on newel posts, bed headboards and garden gate posts and are to be found in a wide variety of sizes, shapes and styles, some being carved, as well as turned, and very elaborate. If your task is to replace a top that has become lost or damaged you may have an original to copy, but if this is not the case a classic ball or acorn shape as described in this chapter may well be suitable.

TURNING A BALL TOP

1. A sphere is quite difficult to turn, and it is wise to make a template first that can be used to check the development of the shape as the turning progresses. A round shape is pleasant to touch and safe, with no sharp spikes or edges, but if the ball is not absolutely round it can look unattractive.

2. Prepare and mount a blank on a screw chuck. To make the top in Fig 156 you will need a blank measuring 6 × 4¼ × 4¼in (152 × 108 × 108mm). After roughing out the cylinder to the diameter required use a turning guide to mark the important lines on the wood to indicate where the cuts are to be made.

3. Most of the turning is done with a spindle

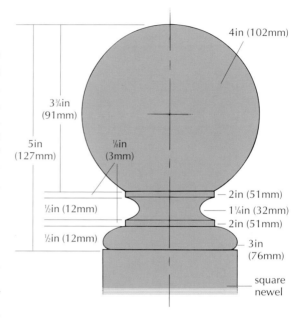

Fig. 156 Ball top for a newel post.

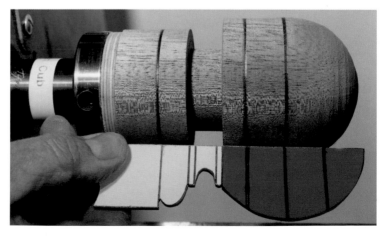

Fig. 157 The partly turned top of the post top sphere and the waist were cut in a blank of mahogany. The turning guide shows the position of the centre-line and other points where cuts will be made. Note the ply spacer that protects the face of the screw chuck.

gouge and a parting tool. Take gentle cuts and check the shape of the sphere regularly against the second half of the turning guide. If tailstock support is needed, a revolving multi-head centre with a cup-shaped end is particularly suitable. A small pad of foam rubber between the sphere being turned and the cup will prevent any marking on the wood.

4. When all the turning is complete, check the ball shape finally against the guide before moving away the toolrest and sanding.

5. If the sphere is to be painted, it is an advantage if the primer can be applied with the work still in position on the lathe, because it is then a simple matter to sand down and denib the primed surface with non-woven web abrasive with the work rotating. The final gloss coat can be painted on when the work has been removed from the lathe.

(Top) *Fig. 158 Use the other half of the turning guide to check that the shape is correctly formed.*

(Above) *Fig. 159 The arrow draws attention to a piece of foam rubber between the work and the cup insert held in the multi-head revolving centre, which will prevent any marking on the surface of the wood. Always use tailstock support when you can, as this will reduce the risk of vibration, especially in a small lathe.*

Fig. 160 The primed ball top ready for gloss painting.

TURNING A SIMPLE ACORN TOP

1. Drill a pilot hole for a screw chuck in a prepared blank of pine or hardwood measuring 4½ × 2¾ × 2¾in (114 × 70 × 70mm). It is usually more satisfactory to drill a slightly smaller pilot hole than normal if you are using pine, because softwood gives more easily and you need to achieve a good, firm grip.

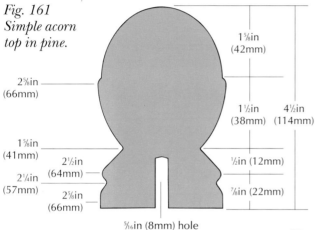

Fig. 161 Simple acorn top in pine.

2⅝in (66mm)

1⅝in (41mm)

2¼in (57mm)

2½in (64mm)

2⅝in (66mm)

1⅝in (42mm)

1½in (38mm)   4½in (114mm)

½in (12mm)

⅞in (22mm)

⁵⁄₁₆in (8mm) hole 1⅛in (28mm) deep

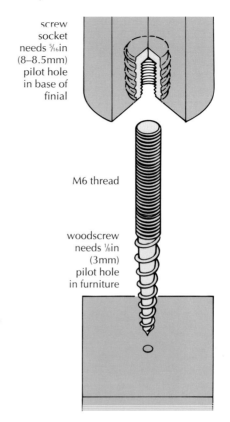

screw socket needs ⁵⁄₁₆in (8–8.5mm) pilot hole in base of finial

M6 thread

woodscrew needs ⅛in (3mm) pilot hole in furniture

Fig. 162 Hanger-bolt system.

2. Figure 163 shows a cross-section of a completed acorn on the screw chuck. The pilot hole has been drilled longer than the length of the chuck screw because it is planned that hanger bolts will be used to secure the acorn to the top of the newel post. A hanger bolt consists of a ¼in (6mm) threaded rod with one end machined as a wood screw. These bolts are used with matching screw sockets, which fit into the hole left by the screw chuck. The wood screw

Fig. 163 A cross-section of a completed acorn on the screw chuck to show a longer hole drilled to take a hanger bolt.

end, below the acorn, is screwed into the top of the newel post. It is very difficult to drill a large hole accurately in the top of a newel post to take an acorn with a spigot, especially if the newel post is already in position. It is much easier to drill a ⅛in (3mm) hole to take the wood screw end of a hanger bolt. The screw socket and bolt will give slightly if the pilot hole is not absolutely true, allowing the base of the acorn to be pulled down flat on to the post. With a large-diameter spigot, if the hole is not absolutely true, the acorn will not seat squarely on top of the post and will look unsightly.

3. Shape the acorn with a spindle gouge, working first from the centre-line towards the tailstock and then from the centre-line towards the headstock.

4. Sand the work with good-quality abrasive. Always remove the toolrest and hold the abrasive under the rotating wood, keeping it moving to prevent lines from forming. The acorn can now be stained to match the newel post, or alternatively a coat of primer can be applied if the acorn is to be painted.

5. Sometimes split acorns are required for half newel posts positioned against the wall. It is dangerous to try to cut an acorn freehand on the bandsaw! First glue the acorn to the end of a long scrap piece of timber using hot-melt glue. Set the bandsaw fence accurately and carefully slice the acorn down the centre. The hot-melt glue will peel off easily.

(Top) *Fig. 164 Sanding the acorn.*

(Middle) *Fig. 165 Comparing two acorns.*

(Bottom) *Fig. 166 Cutting an acorn top in half. Glue the acorn to the end of a scrap piece of timber with hot-melt glue and then pass it through a bandsaw. Note that only the minimum amount of blade is exposed.*

FINIALS

A finial is a decorative top found on clock cases, barometers, and many items of furniture, often in the centre of a broken pediment. It can be made from brass, stone, ivory, wood and other materials, but I am here concerned only with those turned in wood. Finials are vulnerable to damage and are sometimes missing altogether. Although they serve no useful purpose and are purely decorative they do often cover unattractive end grain. As an ornamental decoration it is most important that they should *look* right.

Wooden finials usually fall into one of the following styles: urns with tops; urns with carved flame tops; balls and spikes; elongated and ornate acorns and drops; or upside-down finials.

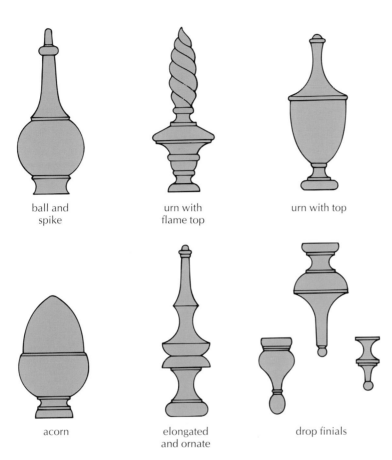

ball and spike

urn with flame top

urn with top

acorn

elongated and ornate

drop finials

Fig. 167 A selection of finial shapes.

Fig. 168 A selection of antique finials. Note that a number have been damaged at the top, where they are most vulnerable.

121

Turning Finials

When turning a replacement finial there are a number of critical design points to be aware of:

- A finial that is too small is worse than no finial at all
- A finial that is too large can appear top-heavy
- Where three finials top an item the centre one is often larger and more ornate than its flanking partners

- Placing an ornate turning on a plain piece of furniture will look wrong, and vice versa
- Most finials have a base or plinth, and if this is too small or abbreviated, the result will not look pleasing
- A shining, highly polished, crisp and new finial on an old and somewhat battered item of furniture will look like an obvious replacement!

TIMBER

It is important to choose the timber you are going to use for the replacement with care; it is best to use the same type of wood as the original if this is at all possible. Many turners collect old wood such as mahogany, oak and beech for renovating purposes, but if this is not available, choose a similar close-grained timber that will turn well. Fruit woods such as pear and cherry are particularly suitable, as is boxwood for very small finials. Pine was often used in the past but modern, fast-grown pine will seldom produce the required result.

FINISHING

Finials may be stained and polished, gilded or painted depending on the original that you are replacing. As ever when repairing or restoring furniture, finishing is the most difficult stage.

FIXING

Most finials are fitted in position by a spigot or dowel with a suitable hole in the host item. Some, however, are fitted with a double-ended iron wood screw or with iron dowels, as, for example, on four-poster beds. I prefer a wooden spigot or dowel but I sometimes do use a proprietary screw socket and hanger bolt system. I have given details of this system already under Post Tops.

A BALL AND SPIKE CLOCK FINIAL

In this typical example, I copied a damaged pine clock finial that had lost its decoration on the top of the spike; it had also been gilded but the finish had worn away. I decided to use boxwood because it is a fine-grain wood that I always enjoy working with, and I finished the new finial in a liquid gold paint.

1. First draw a detailed plan with dimensions. Again, it is worth stressing that this stage is necessary to produce an accurate template.
2. Prepare a blank 6¼ × 2¼ × 2¼in (159 × 57 × 57mm) of fine-grain wood, and centre mark and centre pop one end. Drill a pilot hole to match the screw chuck being used, mount the wood with a spacer in

position on the screw, and screw the chuck on the headstock spindle.

3. Set the lathe speed to 2,000rpm, fit a revolving centre in the tailstock and position the toolrest. Check that the wood revolves without obstruction, and then with a roughing-out gouge turn the blank to a cylinder.

4. Use the template to mark the positions of the three fillets and the bead on the spike, and with a ⅛in (3mm) parting tool cut slots at these five positions to just above the maximum diameters.

5. Form the spike with a sharp spindle gouge, first working at the tailstock end. Take gentle cuts and stop the lathe at

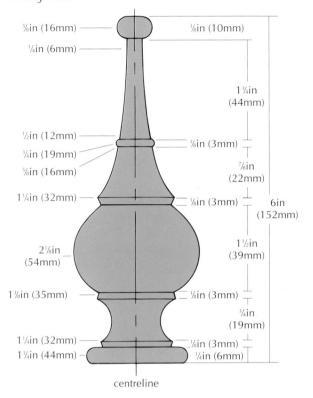

Fig. 169 A ball and spike clock finial.

⅝in (16mm)
¼in (6mm)
⅜in (10mm)
1¾in (44mm)
½in (12mm)
¾in (19mm)
⅝in (16mm)
⅛in (3mm)
⅞in (22mm)
1¼in (32mm)
⅛in (3mm)
6in (152mm)
2⅛in (54mm)
1½in (39mm)
1⅜in (35mm)
⅛in (3mm)
¾in (19mm)
1¼in (32mm)
1¾in (44mm)
⅛in (3mm)
¼in (6mm)

centreline

(Left) Fig. 170 Using the template to mark on the cylinder the positions where slots are to be cut.

Fig. 171 Cutting the slots with a parting tool.

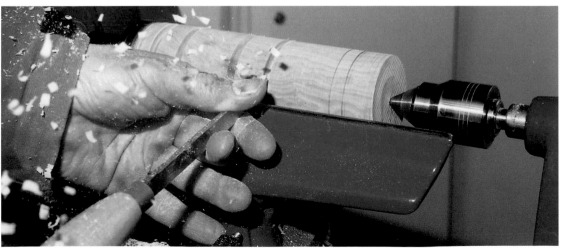

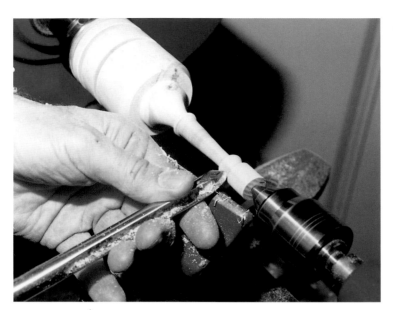

Fig. 172 Forming the spike with a sharp spindle gouge.

Fig. 173 The completed finial.

regular intervals to check the shape and diameters. Do not part off the waste wood at the top of the spike until all turning is complete, so that tailstock support can be provided throughout the turning process. Stop the lathe constantly and check the diameters against the turning guide.

6. Form the ball with a spindle gouge or a skew chisel, always cutting *downhill*.

7. Turn the waist with a spindle gouge and then the foot. Tidy up the fillets with a skew chisel.

8. Part off the waste wood with the long point of a skew chisel and then remove the toolrest and sand and burnish the finial. Any small cracks or knots will need to be filled and sanded before any paint is applied.

9. For finishing I used liquid gold paint purchased from an art shop, and applied it with a brush whilst the finial was still held on the lathe, but, if several matched finials are being produced, it will be easier to finish them off the lathe. Apply several layers of paint and gently rub down the work between each coat. A fine-grain wood such as box will take a really good gold paint finish; more porous woods will need several coats of primer first. The intention is not to simulate brass with its high metallic shine, but to produce a gold leaf appearance with a pleasing lustre.

URN WITH A ROUNDED TOP

This type of finial might be found on a Canterbury or on a display cabinet. A possible design is illustrated in Fig. 174. It is smaller than the ball and spike and is quite complex to turn, especially at the base, but the rounded top is pleasing to look at and to touch. A really good finish off the tool is essential.

The original I copied was turned in old mahogany with a rich brown colour and a very fine grain. I made the replacement from some similar old mahogany, but as it is always difficult to find such a dark wood, staining was necessary. To avoid any wastage I turned up a glue chuck and glued the prepared mahogany on to the chuck with hot-melt glue, then screwcd it on to a small faceplate.

SPLIT TURNING

I define split turning as a technique used to produce a half or quarter turning. The blank to be turned is made up of two or more pieces of wood glued together, which are then separated after turning is complete. Split turnings are usually purely decorative and are frequently missing or damaged. Below are described the turning techniques involved in making four typical examples: split acorns, ball and blade knop moulding, relief decoration and quarter turnings.

SPLIT ACORNS

Split acorns are to be found in a form of decorative moulding that was popular towards the end of the eighteenth century, where the lower part of the moulding is

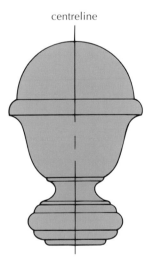

centreline

Fig. 174 An urn-shaped finial with rounded top.

Fig. 175 An urn with a rounded top finial. Note the register marks on the faceplate and on the glue chuck, which guarantee accurate realignment, should this be necessary.

Fig. 176 An example of split turning – an acorn decoration on a bureau. Note the single half acorn to cover the keyhole.

Fig. 177 Gluing the paper in position. The square blank on the left will be turned to form the glue chuck.

fretted out in a series of Gothic arches, often terminating at the bottom of each point with a small half turning that frequently takes the form of an acorn. This type of decoration is to be seen along the top of wardrobes, bookcases and clock hoods, and the actual size of the acorns ranges from small to very small. Occasionally a slightly larger acorn is used on a piece of furniture, or on a door, as a keyhole cover. The acorns were usually turned in a fine-grain wood and stained and polished but sometimes they can be found in a contrasting material, such as ivory. The small half turnings are susceptible to damage, especially on the corners, because they were normally only glued in position.

Turning Split Acorns

1. You will need to create two blanks that are glued together using PVA adhesive and plain paper in a sandwich. This glue, paper, glue sandwich enables the

acorn to be parted when turning is complete, but in the mean time is a strong enough joint to hold the two halves together during the turning process. I am always amazed how effective this simple method is.

2. Hot-melt glue the carefully prepared blank to a piece of thicknessed wood, and screw the wood on to a small screw chuck or faceplate ready for turning. The use of a glue chuck enables the

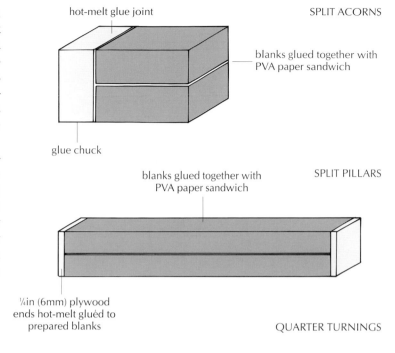

Fig. 178 Split turning.

(Below) *Fig. 179 The turned and polished acorn. Note that the glue chuck has been coloured green. The paper joint can be clearly seen.*

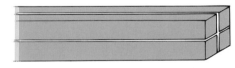

complete blank to be turned and reduces the waste of what may be valuable old timber. It also ensures that, in the case of a screw chuck, the central screw does not force the sandwiched joint apart.

3. After turning and parting off, prise the two halves of the acorn apart with the blade of a pocket knife to be left with two identical split turnings; sand off any remaining paper. It may seem simpler to the reader to turn the acorn from one piece of wood and to saw the completed acorn in half, as I illustrated in the section on post tops, but as these are small turnings it can be very difficult to achieve an accurate cut. However, there are some occasions when the acorn may have to be turned in one and a section cut out, for example if it is to be positioned on a corner.

Fig. 180 Using a penknife to part the two halves carefully.

Fig. 181 Using a beading tool to turn a short length of ball and knop beading.

BALL AND BLADE KNOP BEADING

I recently saw a fine example of ball and blade knop moulding decorating the edge of an antique table, and in my example I have exaggerated its size to show the pattern clearly for the photograph. Again, two lengths of carefully prepared wood are sandwiched together with glue and paper and then turned. Considerable care and practice is required to achieve a uniform pattern. It is difficult to produce over 12in (30cm) in one length because whipping becomes a problem, but it is relatively easy to join shorter lengths, and if you look carefully at this type of decoration on old furniture you will just be able to discern the joins. Remember that small pieces need just as much care as larger turnings and poorly executed mouldings will stand out like a sore thumb!

Fig. 182 Two pieces of prepared wood glued together with paper in between, ready to turn the split columns. Pieces of ¼in (6mm) ply are glued to each end to stop the joint from splitting apart.

Fig. 183 Prising the two halves of the column apart with a penknife.

when pressure is applied from the tailstock. Take care when preparing the wood for the blank and the end pieces to ensure accurate and clean joints. When turning is complete, remove the two plywood ends first and then prise the split turning carefully apart and sand off any remaining paper.

QUARTER TURNINGS

In this example quarter turnings are produced to form simple lengths of beading. This type of moulding is often to be seen on picture and mirror frames, around panels in a door or decorating the top of a trinket box. Hopefully it will only be necessary to replace relatively short lengths, but these will need to match exactly.

Method
1. A quarter turning is made from four pieces of carefully prepared wood. In the example shown I used boxwood and glued together four ¼in (6mm) square pieces as described above to form a ½in (12mm) square blank rather like a Battenburg cake! It is always important not to be in too much of a hurry and to leave the blank cramped up for sufficient time for the glue to cure properly.
2. Fit one cone centre in the headstock and another in the revolving centre held in the tailstock. These cones are

RELIEF DECORATION

Examples of relief decoration can be found on clock cases, fireplaces and cabinets, where half pillars, finials or round shields, for example, are used for adornment.

Split Pillars
The same technique is used as described above, but in this case, because the pillar is to be turned between centres, a piece of ¼in (6mm) plywood is glued at each end of the prepared sandwich to ensure that the two halves of the blank are not forced apart

specifically designed to hold small-section split turnings so that the joints are not forced apart during the turning operation. Then turn the blank to the round with a skew chisel and mark ¼in (6mm) divisions along the whole length of the cylinder.

3. Use a skew or a small beading tool to develop shaped and rounded beads, taking care not to cut in too deep. After sanding and burnishing, remove the work from the lathe and prise the four sections apart with care.

When matching existing beads, the dimensions will have to be taken carefully and the blank marked accordingly so that the replacement fits exactly, or you may find yourself left with half a bead, which will look quite wrong! It is sometimes necessary to make several attempts to get precisely the right result. Be patient!

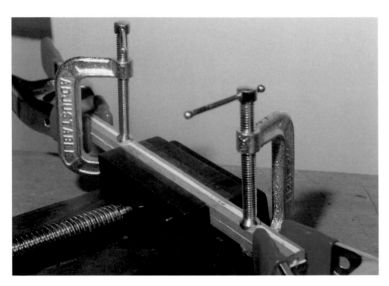

Fig. 184 Four strips of wood glued and cramped up with paper between for quarter turning.

(Below, left) *Fig. 185 Divisions are marked at ¼in (6mm) intervals along the length of the cylinder.*

(Below) *Fig. 186 Shaping beads with a small skew chisel.*

—12—

Models and Games

MODELS

Models, and indeed toys, often do not survive intact for very long. I have restored and made a number of model ships and it is usually the mast, spars and rigging that come to grief. In this particular example I was asked to make a new mast for a rather fine old pond yacht, because the bottom 5in (13cm) had rotted away. This portion of the mast passed through a brass fixing plate on the deck and fitted into a block in the keel. I considered two options: to turn up and splice on a new section of wood to replace the rotten timber and reinforce the join with a steel rod, or to make an entirely new tapered mast. In the end I decided to do both and leave it to the owner to decide which to use! This was how I tackled the two options. Both methods produced good results.

(Above) *Fig. 187 The pond yacht with its new mast.*

Fig. 188 The rotten end of the old mast.

131

SPLICING

1. I selected a piece of straight grain ash, cut a blank 1 × 1 × 7in (25 × 25 × 178mm) and drilled a ¼in (6mm) hole in the blank to a depth of 2in (51mm). The blank was then turned between centres to a cylinder ¾in (19mm) in diameter.
2. The next stage was to take the work off the lathe and, using a disc sander with a mitre guide set at 25 degrees, to sand off the drilled end of the cylinder at an angle of 25 degrees.
3. I cut off the rotten end of the mast and drilled a ¼in (6mm) hole in the cut end to a depth of 2in (51mm). Since it is very difficult to drill a hole accurately in the centre of round stock, a slightly larger hole than the diameter of the reinforcing steel rod was drilled so that the two parts could be aligned accurately. The end of the mast was sanded at an angle of 25 degrees to match the newly turned section.
4. I cut a 3½in (90mm) length of ¼in (6mm) steel rod, which I then glued into the two drilled holes with epoxy resin before binding the joint round with masking tape while the adhesive had set. The epoxy resin filled the gap between the rod and the drilled holes and held the parts firmly in line. Finally, the joint was carefully sanded and the new wood stained to match the old.

A NEW MAST

1. After cutting a piece of straight-grained ash ¾ × ¾ × 50in (19 × 19 × 1,270mm) I then cut a long taper with the bandsaw so that the wood was roughly the shape I needed.
2. I planed off the edges of the blank with a plane and then continued with a low angle block plane. My intention was to get the wood almost round and as smooth as possible, taking care all the time to keep the mast straight and true. Because the mast was too long for my lathe I swivelled the headstock round and made a temporary tailstock from a piece of MDF, with a hole drilled in the centre to take the top end of the mast; this temporary tailstock was held in a vice. Alternatively I could have left the headstock in position and removed the tailstock from the lathe, replacing it with a temporary MDF tailstock supported in a vice on the bench.
3. I placed a small jaw chuck on the lathe and set the lathe speed to 1,250rpm. The partially completed mast was mounted with the bottom end in the chuck and the top end in the temporary tailstock, which was then lubricated with three-in-one oil.

Fig. 189 The top of the mast is held in a temporary home-made tailstock and lubricated with oil.

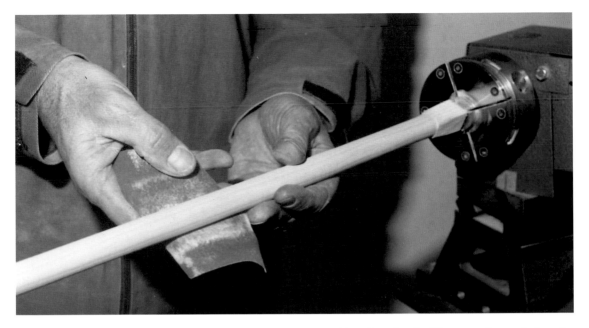

Fig. 190 The foot of the mast is held in the jaws of a combination chuck. The mast is sanded to the correct diameter. Use a hand as a steady to stop the work from flexing.

4. Using one hand as a steady and the other to hold 80 grit abrasive, I started to sand the mast to the round with the work revolving. I gradually worked my way down through the grits to a fine-grade abrasive and finished off with non-woven web abrasive. Every so often I stopped to check the diameter of the mast until the top end measured ¼in (6mm) in diameter and the bottom end ¾in (18mm), and I was happy that there was a uniform taper in between. I found it was necessary to support the mast with a hand until the machine had come to a standstill, otherwise the work flexed to such an extent that there was a possibility that it could break.

5. Leaving the work mounted in the lathe, I stained the ash with antique pine spirit dye to match the original mast and then removed the work from the lathe. When the stain was dry I gave the new mast several coats of clear yacht varnish.

GAMES

It often happens that the simplest of games becomes unusable because a piece is missing. The examples that immediately come to mind are chess pieces, draughtsmen and backgammon pieces. Other games may have turned pegs or counters. Traditionally, most of these games had pieces made of boxwood and ebony to give the required contrast for the opposing sides; more exotic chess sets were once turned in ivory, and can now be made from an ivory alternative (*see* Chapter 13).

The Staunton chess pattern, which was designed by Nathaniel Cook in 1855, and named after his friend the master player Howard Staunton, uses symbols in their plainest form. The design has never been equalled and it has become the recognized standard. I have chosen a Staunton pawn as an example of a missing piece; this may, at first sight, seem the easiest of pieces to

Fig. 191 Chess pawns and draughtsmen.

replicate, but in fact it requires considerable care and skill to achieve precisely the correct shape, especially for the ball on top. Furthermore, because the pawn can easily be compared with the others in the set, one that is too big, for example, will stand out like a sore thumb!

TURNING A REPLACEMENT CHESS PAWN

1. Hot-melt glue a piece of boxwood branch to a glue chuck, and secure it to a small faceplate. A glue chuck is a good choice because it avoids unnecessary waste of an expensive, and sometimes hard to obtain, timber.
2. Turn the blank to the round to just above the maximum diameter of the piece and face off the end.
3. Tackle the ball top first. Take the length of the ball and its diameter from an existing piece and mark these on the blank. Then, with a point tool, form the ball slightly larger than the final size. I used an arm rest, which made this operation easier because the tool can then be controlled by moving the body position very slightly, but the tool and toolrest can be used in the conventional manner.

Size

Chess pieces 3½in (89mm) in height are the most popular size for general play, while a size of 4½in (114mm) size is preferred for competitions.

4. True the ball up to an accurate shape using a piece of brass tubing with a bevel ground on the outside to form a cutting edge on the inside. If you are just making one pawn then brass is hard enough, but if you plan to make several, a steel tube would keep its edge longer. Move the tube into the rotating, partly finished ball and move it gently from side to side. With a little practice, a really accurate sphere results. It is worth trying out such a technique on a scrap piece of wood before attempting it on an actual piece. It must be stressed that the sphere should be shaped as true as possible with turning tools before finishing off with the tube.
5. The remainder of the turning is relatively straight forward but the diameters

Fig. 192 *Rounding the top of the chess pawn using a brass tube.*

of the various parts do need to be checked very carefully with the original and, as with all intricate small work, it pays to carry out the turning in gentle stages. If you are not satisfied with the final result, be brave, throw it in the bin and start again! For black pieces, if ebony is not available, boxwood can be stained successfully, and there are plenty of products to choose from to do this.

Fig. 193 *Checking measurements with Vernier callipers.*

TURNING A DRAUGHTSMAN

1. To make a light-coloured piece, cut a suitable blank of English boxwood and hot-melt glue it to a glue chuck secured to a faceplate. Turn the blank to the required diameter and face off the end.
2. A card turning guide helps to make sure that the decorative pattern of rings will match the rest of the set. Mark the positions off in pencil on the smooth, faced-off surface of the blank.
3. Turn the rings using a parting tool and a small beading tool. Once you are happy with the pattern, burnish the work very gently, and part off the piece with a thin parting tool, allowing a little extra in thickness. If there is enough wood left on the blank to produce a few more pieces, you will finish up with several

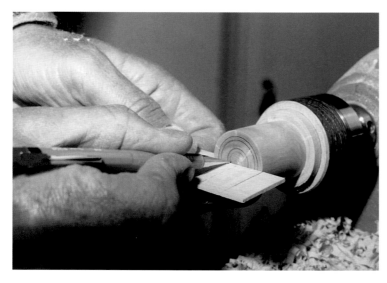

Fig. 194 Using a guide to mark the positions of the decorative rings.

Fig. 195 Parting off the part-turned draughtsman with a thin parting tool.

draughts turned on one side only with a rough, unfinished reverse side.

4. The next task is to make a jam chuck from a piece of scrap hardwood with a recess of about ⅛in (3mm) in depth and sufficient diameter to hold the partly turned draughtsman in a good, tight grip. Before making such a chuck it is as well to consider how the work is going to be removed after turning is completed! The lathe I used had a hollow headstock spindle and the faceplate also had a hole

Fig. 196 Using a jam chuck to hold a draughtsman.

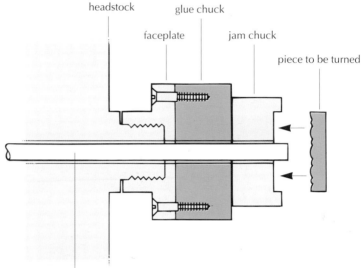

(Below)
Fig. 197 The partly turned work is reversed and pushed into the prepared jam chuck. Note the hole in the centre of the jam chuck, which enables a bar to be pushed through the rear of the headstock spindle to remove the completed piece from the chuck.

passing a dowel rod through a hollow headstock spindle, faceplate and a drilled glue chuck and jam chuck, enables a piece to be removed from the jam chuck without damage

Fig. 198 Cutting the decorative rings on the reverse side with the tool supported on the arm rest.

Fig. 199 Knocking out the finished draughtsman by pushing a rod through the headstock spindle, faceplate, glue chuck and jam chuck.

in its centre. By drilling a hole through the centre of the jam chuck and glue chuck I was able to pass a dowel rod through the headstock spindle, faceplate, glue chuck and jam chuck and push out the finished pieces without any damage. Unfortunately, some lathes do not have a hollow headstock, which means that the faceplate will have to be removed from the lathe to enable the dowel to be passed through the back.

5. With the half-completed blank secure in the jam chuck, turn the reverse side to match the obverse, burnish it and remove it from the chuck.

Holding Playing Pieces

It is possible to use more sophisticated chucking systems, but the jam chuck is cheap, simple and free from any sharp edges. This method of holding ensures that the outside edges of the turned work are not marked or damaged by metal chuck jaws. A backgammon piece can be turned in exactly the same way.

—13—

Unusual Items

ALTERNATIVE MATERIALS

Synthetic ivory substitute and other alternative materials to simulate abalone, mother-of-pearl, horn and tortoiseshell, are all available. They are produced in a modern polyester resin in rods of different diameters. These natural materials are now protected and unobtainable, but the alternative materials work well. Synthetic ivory, for example, has a grained appearance very similar to the real thing.

The material turns well but scrapers should be used rather than gouges and skews; with a little practice very good results can be achieved. During turning, masses of thin shavings are created, which are static and tend to cling to the lathe; the material is non-toxic and not unpleasant to use, but it is wise to vacuum up the shavings frequently because the material is flammable.

Alternative ivory is very useful in repair work for replacing small knobs, missing ivory chess pieces, counters and pegs, for example. Not only does the material turn well, but it can also be filed to form more complex shapes. Small ivory knobs are often found on miniature chests of drawers, internal desk drawers, collector's cabinets and on similar small items of furniture. When originally made in real ivory the stem and the top of the knob were

Fig. 200 Knobs and a chess piece turned in alternative ivory.

made in two separate pieces and then screwed together with a thread cut in the ivory. Clearly this was done to avoid wasting such a valuable and rare material, but in the following instructions the replacement is turned in one piece.

TURNING A SMALL KNOB IN ALTERNATIVE IVORY

1. Choose a diameter of rod as near to the size required as possible to keep any wastage to the minimum. Cut the rod to

Fig. 201 Cutting a blank of alternative ivory rod with a mitre saw. Note that the blank is held with a G-cramp for safety and accuracy.

Fig. 202 Do not be tempted to cut a round rod with a bandsaw!

the desired length with a mitre saw and make sure that the cut end is absolutely true. Do not attempt to cut small pieces with a bandsaw!

2. Hold the rod firmly in a drill chuck mounted in the headstock, set the lathe speed at 2,000rpm and position the toolrest close to the work.

3. Use a point tool, which has three facets, to turn the top dome of the knob and then form any pattern required. Shape the underside with small, round-nosed scrapers. Hone off the burr of the scraper and keep the tool edge sharp. Hold the handle of the tool up, with the cutting edge just below the centre line, and gently move the tool into the material.

4. Form the spigot with a small beading tool or a parting tool.

5. Polish the finished knob with metal polish as it rotates in the lathe. Alternatively you can buff the knob with a polishing mop, held on an arbor on the lathe, or on another power unit. Alternative ivory can be darkened to give an aged

(Above) *Fig. 203 The alternative ivory blank held in a drill chuck. A point tool is being used to shape the flange.*

Fig. 204 Buffing up an alternative ivory chess piece on a polishing wheel using a polishing compound.

effect by soaking it in a solution of tea, and it can also be stained successfully using dyes.

REPAIRING A SPINNING WHEEL

Spinning wheels were very common at one time in rural areas. Now they are more likely to be seen in museums or as rather trendy ornaments. The wheel itself can be one of two types of construction: the **hooped ring**, in which the rim is made from bent wood that has been steamed and formed round a mould, or the **jointed wheel**, which is made up from four segments of wood, jointed and glued together and then turned. It is the latter type of wheel that I am looking at in this chapter.

'Perhaps you would like to have a go at this …', a friend said, thrusting a cardboard box at me full of broken spinning wheel parts. On closer examination it was evident that although most of the frame could be restored, the wheel itself was beyond repair; fortunately there were enough pieces left to enable me to produce an accurate drawing.

I did some research and it seemed that my spinning wheel was a Low Irish or Dutch wheel, which would have been used to spin flax. It was during the 1800s that spinning wheels of this type were distributed by district boards in Ireland so that the very poor could make some money, and they cost 12½ pence each! I like to think that my broken spinning wheel was from this period, but there is no real way of telling.

The principles and techniques involved in making this wheel can be applied to wheels other than spinning wheels and I found it an interesting and absorbing exercise. For the purposes of making the new wheel, it could be divided up into three distinct areas: the rim, the hub and the twelve spokes.

Fig. 205 The broken oak wheel for repair. Note that the rim is badly affected by woodworm and that there are only six spokes left.

THE RIM

1. I made the wheel rim from four half-jointed segments of oak, ¾in (19mm) thick, to give a 6½in (165mm) outer radius and a 5in (127mm) inner radius. A cardboard template was used for marking out the thicknessed oak. The basic shape was cut out using a fretsaw and the half-joints were cut by hand with a tenon saw. The four segments were then glued up and cramped to a thick piece of MDF to ensure that no twisting occurred. Once dry, each joint was reinforced with two ¼in (6mm) wooden dowels to give extra strength.

2. I took a piece of 1in (25mm) thick MDF and cut a disc 13in (330mm) across, using a powered fretsaw. I intended to use a combination indexed chuck with a screw chuck insert, and so I drilled a ⁵⁄₁₆in (8mm) hole right through the centre and secured the disc on the chuck in the headstock. It was necessary to swivel the headstock round on my lathe to give

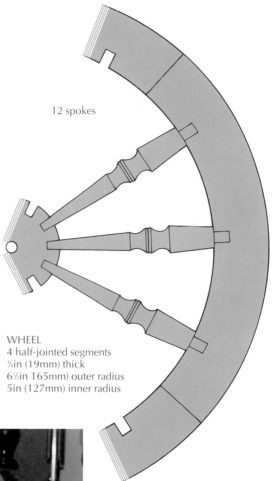

12 spokes

WHEEL
4 half-jointed segments
¾in (19mm) thick
6½in 165mm) outer radius
5in (127mm) inner radius

(Above) *Fig. 206 A spinning wheel: the wheel rim, the hub and the spokes.*

Fig. 207 The wheel rim has been hot-melt glued to the MDF disc and turned. You can see the centre screw from the screw chuck. The lathe headstock is swivelled round.

143

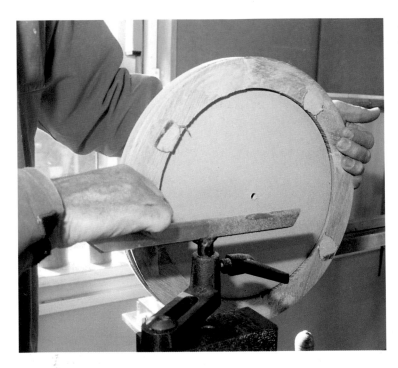

Fig. 208 The MDF disc has been cut to form a jam chuck and the wheel rim has been reversed and pushed on so that the second side can be turned to match the first. The remains of the glue can easily be removed with the turning tool.

sufficient clearance. The prepared oak rim was then glued on to the MDF with four blobs of equally spaced hot-melt glue with a curing time of 60 seconds. Remember that MDF dust is deemed to be harmful, so it is a wise precaution to wear a mask when cutting, sanding or turning it.

3. I set the lathe speed to 450rpm and turned the rim as follows. The front surface was first gently turned with a spindle gouge, and two decorative grooves cut with a point tool. The inside of the rim was turned true with a spindle gouge and finished off with a sharp beading tool. The outer rim was also turned true and two shallow grooves were cut with a spindle gouge for the driving band. The rim was then sanded and burnished and gently eased off the MDF with a thin knife blade.

4. I then formed a jam chuck from the MDF disc left on the lathe to hold the inside of the partly turned rim, so that

the reverse side could be turned. This was done by cutting away an area on the MDF disc to make a jam chuck about 10in (254mm) in diameter with a depth of ¼in (6mm). The cuts were made with a parting tool, and I took care not to take away too much material, so that when the wheel rim was pushed on there was a good tight fit. The wheel rim was then turned to match the first side.

5. The next task was to use some form of indexing system to mark accurately the twelve positions on the wheel for the spokes. Some lathes have a built-in indexing facility but mine does not. I used an indexed chuck with twenty-four divisions, and marked every second hole on the chuck in colour as shown in the photograph. Indexing holes are not usually numbered and it is easy to lose count! If you do not have an indexing facility then twelve equally spaced positions can be marked out with the aid of a protractor. First I made a pencil mark

on the MDF opposite each position on the wheel rim where a hole was to be drilled. The wheel, still held on the jam chuck, was removed from the lathe and the twelve pencil marks were transferred to the inside of the rim and each mark was punched. I then removed the wheel from the jam chuck and drilled the holes to a depth of ⅜in (10mm) at each of the punched positions, in the centre of the rim, with a ¼in (6mm) drill bit fitted in a small cordless drill.

(Above) *Fig. 209 Every other hole on the indexed chuck has been marked with a red sticker to give twelve positions. The photograph shows the arm that locates in each of the indexed holes to hold the position accurately.*

(Above, right) *Fig. 210 An accurate mark is made on the MDF disc at the twelve positions, and these are then transferred to the inside of the rim.*

Fig. 211 This small cordless drill enables me to drill the holes inside the rim, at the centre. Note the yellow tape that acts as a depth guide.

THE HUB

This was an interesting piece of turning. Not only did the hub need to have a hole through its centre, it also needed twelve holes, equally spaced, around the circumference to hold the ends of the spokes. It also had to part into two identical halves because the inner ends of the spokes were to be glued on one half of the hub and then the second half was to be glued on top.

1. The hub was turned from an oak blank 3 × 3 × 4½in (76 × 76 × 114mm). Again I used the indexed chuck with a screw chuck insert, and turned the blank to a diameter of 2½in (64mm). The outer end was faced off with a spindle gouge. A ⁵⁄₁₆in (8mm) drill was fitted in a drill chuck, mounted in the tailstock, and a centre hole was drilled to a depth of 3in (76mm).

2. I drew a line around the circumference of the blank, 1¼in (32mm) in from the

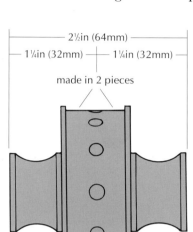

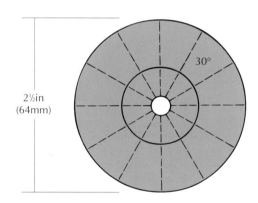

Fig. 212 Plan for the spinning wheel hub.

Fig. 213 The two faced-off surfaces are glued together with paper in between to form a blank for the hub. The paper joint will allow part A and part B to be easily separated when turning is complete. Note the rough surface at the end, which is left by the parting tool after parting the blank prior to reversing B.

outer edge, and with a thin parting tool cut right through on the line. I now had part A and part B. Using a spindle gouge I faced off the end of part A so that it was absolutely flat. Part B was then reversed and glued to A with a paper/PVA sandwich so that the two faced-off surfaces were glued together with a sheet of paper in between. The tailstock was fitted with a revolving centre, and this was brought up to act as a cramp while the glue set.

3. Using the index facility on the chuck and a drilling jig, I drilled twelve equally spaced holes, to a depth of ⅜in (10mm), round the circumference of the hub along the paper joint. The drilling jig was then replaced with a toolrest, and the hub was turned to shape with a spindle gouge.

4. After sanding and burnishing, the hub was parted off at the headstock with a thin parting tool. Parts A and B were then gently prised apart and the remaining paper sanded off.

Fig. 214 The holes are drilled around the circumference of the hub with the aid of a jig, which holds the drill bit square to the wood to be drilled and prevents it from wandering. Note the arm with the pin located in one of the holes in the indexed chuck.

Fig. 215 Once turning on the hub is complete, part A and part B are carefully prised apart with a knife.

THE SPOKES

1. This was the easy part! I first prepared twelve blanks ¾ × ¾ × 5¼in (19 × 19 × 133mm) and turned them all to ⅝in (16mm) round.
2. I made a cardboard turning guide to ensure that all the spokes would end up exactly the same, and mounted and turned each in turn. To produce identical shapes it is important to follow the same sequence and use the same tools each time!

ASSEMBLY

1. I found it useful to use the MDF jam chuck as a jig to position the spokes

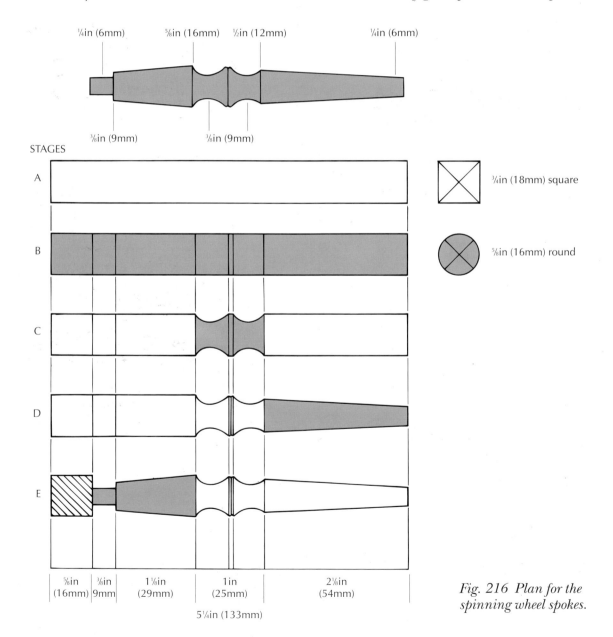

Fig. 216 Plan for the spinning wheel spokes.

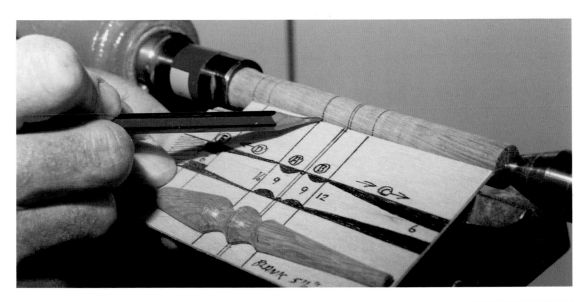

(Above) *Fig. 217 Marking on the turned blank the lines where the cuts are to be made to form the shape of the spoke. The guide shows a half-section made from the prototype. Note that the guide also shows all the relevant measurements. Using a guide like this will ensure that all the spokes end up the same.*

Fig. 218 It is particularly important that the spigot, which goes into the hub, is the correct size. It is worth taking the trouble to make a little measuring gauge for this purpose.

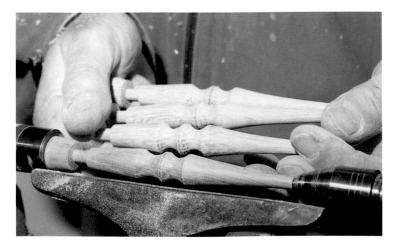

(Left) *Fig. 219 Comparing the spokes with one just completed that is still on the lathe. The waste wood at the headstock end will be cut off with a fine saw.*

Fig. 220 A dry run to see that the spokes all fit in the rim and in the hub. Before gluing up takes place, all remnants of the paper joint will be sanded off.

(Right) *Fig. 221 Drawing of a Low Irish or Dutch flax wheel.*

(Below) *Fig. 222 The completed wheel.*

correctly. I glued three blocks of scrap wood into the jig to raise the wheel rim higher and inserted a wooden dowel in the centre hole to act as a locating guide for the hub.

2. I placed part A of the hub on the centre dowel spigot. I tried a dry run, positioning the spokes first into the rim and then into the hub, and glued them into position when I was satisfied. Finally I glued part B of the hub on top of A and cramped up the two parts. The wheel was complete!

— Appendix —

Safety When Woodturning

Woodturners are vulnerable to accidents and health problems, but, by being aware of the dangers, and by practising sensible habits, they can reduce the risks greatly. The hazards they must be aware of are: damage to the respiratory system from fine wood dust, damage to eyes and skin, and physical damage to the body, in particular the hands. The dangers of electrocution and fire in the workshop must also be recognized.

THE WORKSHOP

The electrical system in the workshop must be sound. If there is any doubt at all, a professional electrician should be consulted. The lathe must be correctly wired, preferably with an NVR (no volt release) switch. If the workshop is in a damp garage or shed, a double pole protector plug (residual current circuit breaker) is a wise investment.

Lighting is most important and natural light is preferable. Tube lighting can produce a strobe effect, giving the impression that the work is not turning.

The workshop needs to be warm. Cold hands are stiff and clumsy and more vulnerable to knocks and grazing. The type of heating needs to be selected with care. Radiant electric fires, open-element convector heaters, fan heaters and paraffin heaters are not suitable as they clog with sawdust and so present a fire risk. A heater with enclosed heating tubes or an oil-filled radiator would be suitable.

Some workshops may have a wood burner. Sweep up regularly to keep the floor free of shavings and clear sawdust from the bench. Try to avoid a build-up of dust by cleaning and vacuuming regularly. A dust extractor can be an expensive machine to buy and some are really only chip collectors. There has recently been a great deal written about the danger of wood dust to the nose and lungs, so no woodworker can afford to be complacent about this problem. If you are going to do a lot of turning an extractor will be necessary; the very least every turner should do is to wear a disposable dust mask that complies with the European standard EN 149 FFP 1 or 2, and this should be worn during the turning *and* the cleaning-up process. An airflow helmet is another, more expensive, alternative.

Make it a rule not to smoke, eat or drink in the workshop.

EYES AND SKIN

You *must* wear eye protection. Spectacles alone are not sufficient unless they have been specially designed for industrial use. Goggles are inexpensive and effective, but a full-face visor, costing a little more, will give both eyes and face protection from flying wood chips and dust. Eye protection and the wearing of a dust mask is equally important when you are sharpening chisels on a bench grinder.

I also find it worth while to apply barrier cream to my hands before starting to prepare timber. Some woods are toxic and can cause skin rashes and irritation. Personally, I have found some boxwoods and walnuts give me an irritant rash, so I treat them with great caution.

After a woodturning session where a lot of sawdust has been created it is advisable to change out of your working clothes and to have a shower to remove dust from the hair, scalp and skin

THE LATHE AND EQUIPMENT

A lathe revolves at high speeds, so long hair or loose clothing can become caught up in a matter of split seconds. Tie back long hair and wear a proper smock with tight cuffs; sweaters quickly become impregnated with dust and are not recommended.

The lathe must be firmly mounted on a bench or stand. The height of the lathe and the position and stance of the turner are not strictly safety factors, but long hours working in an awkward position can result in back and neck problems, so the ergonomics need to be considered. The centre height, just below elbow height, is a good starting point; however, the important thing is that you should feel comfortable.

Some three-jaw and four-jaw chucks have nasty edges where the jaws protrude beyond the body of the chuck. This type of chuck should always be protected with a guard, but they seldom are. The need for a guard applies equally to some home-made chucks – those using jubilee clips, for example. The knuckles are particularly vulnerable when the chuck is revolving at high speed.

Lathe tools should be hung firmly and neatly and replaced after use. Spring clips are not always reliable; it is better to make a hardwood racking system to suit each individual chisel and gouge. Avoid placing tools on a shelf below the lathe bed when you are working. Sharp tools tend to become buried in shavings and fingers can be cut when rummaging to find them. Sometimes the vibration from the lathe causes a chisel to fall off and stab the turner's foot!

The turner is well advised to invest in a proprietary bench grinder on which the grindstones are all partially encased in guards. An unguarded grindstone, on an old motor or electric drill, can be very dangerous, since bits of the stone can fly in all directions, or, at worst, the stone can disintegrate with dire results. I repeat, do not forget to wear your eye protection and your dust mask when grinding.

It is essential that your tools are sharp and have good handles. Blunt tools can increase the risk of a serious dig-in, while cracked and damaged handles can result in disaster. I do not like home-made turning chisels made from old files – I have seen the short tangs fracture with interesting results! It is really worth buying good-quality tools that have been designed and manufactured for turning. Remember to treat all edge tools with respect and keep them sharp.

PREPARING TO TURN

The preparation of the timber depends on the holding system to be used. Whatever system you use to hold your wood in the lathe make sure it is held firmly. Look out for faults or cracks in the timber, and ensure that your chucks are well maintained. The aim is make sure that the timber does not fly off and cause injury to the turner.

When the workpiece has been safety secured in the lathe, the toolrest should be set to suit the work and the tool to be used. Avoid working close to the end of a rest and ensure that the work will rotate freely. The lathe should always be off when any adjustments are being made. If your lathe does not have an NVR switch, fit a separate isolating switch or unplug it while carrying out alterations.

The next consideration is the speed to be selected. Many serious accidents occur because the speed of the lathe is too high for the work being turned. Remember, the larger the work, the slower the speed. I usually reset the lathe to a slow speed at the end of a turning session.

TURNING

If at this stage the turner is uncertain which tool to use and is new to woodturning, I suggest that they sign up for a woodturning course. Poor technique and lack of a basic understanding of how to use turning tools will increase the risk of an accident. Even if you are a confident turner, you should always think about what you are doing, use the correct, sharp tool for the job and stop the lathe if you hear a change in sound to determine the cause.

You will need to adjust the toolrest as the diameter of the work reduces. To carry out this operation, or any other adjustment to any part of the machine, *always* stop the lathe first. You must also stop the lathe when you wish to use measuring callipers.

There is a temptation as the work progresses to reach out and feel the revolving work. Beware of sharp corners and knife-like edges. Do not use your fingers to clear dust from places such as the inside of a revolving box – always stop the machine first.

DRILLING

There are a number of drilling techniques that can be used on the lathe, but great care is needed. Drills have a habit of binding in the work, and if the turner is holding the work accidents can happen. The turner should never rely solely on his hands to hold the work being drilled.

SANDING

This is a dusty operation, so make sure you wear a disposable dust mask, a respirator or an air-flow helmet. Before sanding always remove the toolrest and move the tool holder out of the way. Hold the abrasive *under* the work so that if it grabs it will move away from you. Do not wrap the abrasive material around your fingers. Take particular care with steel wool, which can cause nasty abrasions if you lose control of it. If possible, use a modern product such as non-woven web abrasive, which is much better.

POLISHING

The basic rule in polishing is to watch out for a cloth wrap-around. As with abrasives, do not wrap the polishing cloth round a finger before applying it to the rotating work. Should the cloth wrap round the work, your finger will go with the cloth! Use the cloth as a pad under the work. I prefer to use kitchen paper, which will just tear and disintegrate if it is caught. Liquid polishes applied to the revolving work will fly all over the place, so again you will need eye protection. Stains, polishes and adhesives often have strong fumes that are harmful and unpleasant to inhale, so these should be used in a well-ventilated workshop. These products are also often highly inflammable and should be stored carefully.

ENDING A TURNING SESSION

At the end of the turning session, the follow actions should become routine:

1. Unplug the machine if no NVR switch is fitted.
2. Remove the toolrest.
3. Set the lathe to a slow speed.
4. Sharpen the tools used during the session.
5. Put away all tools and accessories.

6. Clean the lathe and working area, keeping a mask on during the process.
7. Remove your turning smock and leave it in the workshop. Place disposable mask in a plastic box ready to be used again. Recharge airflow helmet if necessary.
8. Shower to remove dust from hair, scalp and skin.

VISITORS

Should you have visitors in your workshop whilst you are working, they too will need eye and lung protection. Never leave any machine running unattended. Make sure that switches are well out of the way of children. I do not encourage watchers while I am working, as they are invariably inquisitive and tend to fiddle with everything in sight! This causes distraction and eventually irritation!

Your woodturning may be only a hobby, but safety precautions should still be taken. The reader will only too often see professional woodturners and demonstrators disregarding the basic safety rules, and this sets a bad example to the amateur woodturner. If good habits are cultivated they will become second nature and risky short cuts will not be taken. Safety precautions may seen pedantic and a boring consideration when turning, but damaged hands could stop you turning for some time and damaged eyes or lungs could stop you turning for ever.

Safety Checklist

1. Do you always wear eye protection for turning, sanding, polishing and grinding?

2. Do you always wear a dust mask when turning, sanding or grinding?

3. Do you wear a smock or similar garment, remove rings and jewellery, and tie back hair if necessary?

4. Do you make it a rule never to smoke, eat or drink in the workshop?

5. Do you routinely inspect the electrical leads and switches on your machines?

6. Do you ensure that your timber is mounted securely and check that it can rotate without obstruction before starting to turn?

7. Do you keep your chisels and gouges sharp?

8. Do you put your turning tools away after use?

9. Do you always stop the machine before making any alternations?

10. Do you remove the toolrest and move the tool holder out of the way when sanding?

11. Are you aware of the risks of wrap-around when sanding and polishing?

12. Do you use chuck guards?

13. Do you leave your lathe set on a low speed at the end of a working session?

14. Do you keep the workshop as clean as possible?

15. Do you keep visitors to your workshop under control?

Glossary

Acorn finial a turned decoration used on clock cases, chairs and furniture and shaped to resemble an acorn

Arris sharp edge where two planes or curved surfaces meet, often used to describe the sharp edge on the side of a turning tool

Baluster a short pear-shaped pillar or post supporting the handrail of a staircase

Baluster shape a peardrop form with the widest section at the bottom

Balustrade a row of balusters supporting a rail or parapet

Bead a half round convex moulding, its surface being either flat with the adjacent surface or raised above it

Beading tool a turning tool of square section with two bevels used to form beads

Bun foot a ball-shaped foot usually greater in diameter than height

Cove a hollow or concave moulding

Drop finial a turned decoration which hangs downwards

Dowel a round wooden rod sometimes used for jointing

Exotic wood rare imported woods such as ebony, kingwood, tulip wood, olivewood, cocobolo and pink ivory

Ferrule a metal collar to fit on a spigot to stop wood splitting, e.g. tool handle

Fillet a narrow, flat, band between mouldings

Finial a turned, decorative, ornamental top for chairs, clocks, beds, barometers etc. Can be made of wood, ivory, stone or metal

Faceplate a metal plate which screws on to the headstock and on to which a blank of wood can be secured with woodscrews

Fruitwood timber from a fruit tree such as pear, apple, cherry etc.

Gilding process of applying gold leaf to a wood surface

Hardwood timber from a broad-leaf tree such as oak, lime, sycamore, ash etc.

Knop a small decorative shape on a spindle

Mould a shape used to emphasize the change from one curve to another

Newel centre pillar of winding stair; corner or end-post of stair-rail

Patina unique colour of wood finish resulting from age, polish and everyday handling

Quirk a sunken groove at the side of a bead and fillet

Softwood timber from a needle-bearing tree such as pine or yew

Turning guide gives the position of change of shape, fillets, coves, and beads on an item to be turned

Turning template a female guide which can be used to check the shape of an item being turned

Index